Twayne's United States Authors Series

EDITOR OF THIS VOLUME

Mason Lowance

University of Massachusetts

Cotton Mather

TUSAS 328

Cotton Mather

COTTON MATHER

By BABETTE M. LEVY
Hunter College

TWAYNE PUBLISHERS
A DIVISION OF G. K. HALL & CO., BOSTON

Published in 1979 by Twayne Publishers,
A Division of G. K. Hall & Co.
All Rights Reserved

Printed on permanent/durable acid-free paper and bound
in the United States of America

First Printing

Library of Congress Cataloging in Publication Data

Levy, Babette May, 1907 -
Cotton Mather.

(Twayne's United States authors series)
Bibliography: p. 169 - 85
Includes index.
1.   Mather, Cotton, 1663 - 1728—Criticism and
interpretation.
PS805.Z5L4   973.2'092'4 [B]   78 - 23445
ISBN 0-8057-7261-8

In memory of the courage, goodness, and integrity of
Babette M. Levy

Contents

About the Author

Babette M. Levy, the first Charles A. Dana Professor of English at Sweet-Briar College, who held that post from her appointment in 1968 until her retirement in 1973, died December 21, 1977, in Huntington, New York, after a long illness. She was a leading scholar of Colonial America, and, in addition to many articles and reviews, had written *Preaching in the First Half Century of New England History* (1942) and *Early Puritanism in the Southern and Island Colonies* (1960) Babette Levy was a 1928 graduate of Hunter College, where she taught from 1929 to 1966. She held the M.A. degree (1929) and Ph.D. (1942) from Columbia University, and another M.A. in Librarianship (1961) from the University of Denver. In 1967 - 68, she held an appointment as Distinguished Visiting Professor of English at Morehouse College in Atlanta. In 1942, Professor Levy was awarded the Brewer Prize, given by the American Society of Church History, for the best manuscript submitted in a national competition. She also held two grants from the Institute of Early American History and Culture in Williamsburg. The manuscript for *Cotton Mather* was completed in its entirety before her death, and has been published exactly as she submitted it in 1977.

Preface

Before Babette Levy died, she submitted a typescript of her book on Cotton Mather to Twayne Publishers. The editors have not altered the work in any way, except to change the occasional and obvious typographical error. The study of Mather's life and writing are hers, and we have not attempted to revise her final version. This document was complete in every detail belonging to the Twayne format: chronology, narrative, bibliography, and notes. Therefore what follows is Babette Levy's study of Cotton Mather exactly as she wished to have it published.

For a treatment of Cotton Mather's life and writing, it is neither exhaustive nor comprehensive, nor was it intended to be. Babette Levy was a teacher, primarily of undergraduates, and her study of Mather is written for them—an extension of her life-long efforts as a teacher of Colonial America, and a form of teaching in the very best sense of the word. References are included to works of scholarship that examine specific aspects of Cotton Mather's thinking, e.g., his writings on typology and historiography. Babette Levy's book is designed to provide a sound introduction to the life and mind of Cotton Mather, best known of that New England dynasty whose name is synonymous with Puritanism. It is a welcome and valuable addition to the Twayne United States Authors Series.

Babette Levy left no immediate survivors, though she will long be remembered by scores of students she has taught and by her colleagues in the field of Colonial American Literature. Her early study of New England preaching is a classic example of pioneering scholarship and research, and her human qualities are best summarized by her god-daughter, Mrs. Bernard Meoli, who authored the dedication of this volume. In her final struggle against a terminal illness, she taught us not only how to face death, but also the importance of dedication to those living principles and interests that each of us values. This book was written during the period of that struggle, the final achievement of a committed teacher and scholar who loved her work and left us all richer for her contributions to the field.

MASON I. LOWANCE, JR.
Field Editor, Twayne Publishers

Amherst, Massachusetts

Chronology

Americana published in London; his wife, Abigail, died December 5 after a long illness.

1703   Married, August 18, Elizabeth (Clark) Hubbard, widow, daughter of the well-known scholar Dr. John Clark.

1704   Daughter Elizabeth born July 13.

1706   Wrote *The Negro Christianized* and numerous other appeals urging the Christianizing of Negro slaves; son Samuel (second of name) born October 30.

1708   Delivered one of the first temperance sermons, *Sober Considerations.*

1709   Son Nathaniel born May 16, died November 24.

1710   Published *Bonifacius. An Essay upon the Good, that is to be Devised and Designed by Those Who Desire . . . to Do Good,* his most reprinted work (usually under the title *Essays to do Good*); received degree of Doctor of Divinity from the University of Glasgow.

1711   Daughter Jerusha born April 1.

1712   Began letters to the Royal Society on natural phenomena in America (*Curiosa Americana,* 1712 - 1724).

1713   Elected a Fellow of the Royal Society; twin children Martha and Eleazer born October 30; during an epidemic of measles his wife, Elizabeth, died November 9; Eleazer, midnight November 17/18; Martha, November 20; Jerusha, November 21.

1715   Married, July 5, Lydia (Lee) George, widow, daughter of the Reverend Samuel Lee.

1716   Daughter Katherine, ill with consumption, died December 16.

1717   Published *Malachi. Or, The Everlasting Gospel, Preached unto the Nations,* a strong plea for tolerance; instrumental in the establishing of Yale College.

1718   Published *Psalterium Americanum. The Book of Psalms . . . in Blank Verse;* forced to recognize that his third wife had periods of insanity.

1720   Published *The Christian Philosopher* (London, 1720, postdated 1721), his reconciliation of religion and natural science.

1721   Advocated and managed to start inoculation for smallpox, despite medical opposition; daughter Abigail (Mather) Willard died with her newborn baby September 21.

1723   The Rev. Increase Mather, his father and colleague, died August 23.

1724   Benjamin Franklin visited him; learned August 20 of the death by drowning of his son Increase.

1726   Published *Ratio Disciplinae Fratrum Nov Anglorum* (first written in 1701 and revised from time to time subsequently), an attempt to preserve the discipline of New England's first Congregational churches by an "Account of the Methods and Customs in our Churches" that remained the standard text for a hundred years; and *Manuductio ad Ministerium: Directions for a Candidate of the Ministry;* daughter Elizabeth (Mather) Cooper died August 7.

1727   Seriously ill during the early and latter part of the year.

1728   Died February 13; buried in the family tomb, Copps' Hill Cemetery, Boston.

CHAPTER 1

Personal Life of the "Principal Ornament of This Country"[1]

None goes to Heaven on a Feather-bed. (Mather, 1714)

C OTTON MATHER[2] was born on February 12, 1663, the eldest son of the Reverend Increase Mather, who was not only the son of New England's revered Richard Mather but who was to become distinguished in his own right as Boston's leading minister and most famous preacher, ruling fellow and then president of Harvard College, and for years powerful consultant of the colony's rulers; and of Maria (Cotton) Mather, the daughter of another of New England's most respected ministers, John Cotton. The honor—and duty—that went with being Increase's son loomed large in the years of Cotton's youth, but even more impressive were the connotations that went with being the grandson of the Reverend Richard Mather and of the Reverend John Cotton. In a Puritan society that had the utmost respect for its clergy, these two men of the first generation of settlers ranked high as English university graduates, renowned preachers in both England and New England, martyrs who had put their faith above the security and comfort of living in their mother country, and guiding lights in the troubled times of the establishment of the colony's churches.

The little boy so grandly named in their honor never could forget what was expected of him as their descendant, and it seemed to him that the eyes of his world were always on him, comparing, contrasting him with previous generations. He lived long enough to know that there were men in a changing society who mocked him for his very efforts to be worthy of his name. The most painful jibe of all was for his defamers to give this esteemed name to their slaves, publicly set at the most menial tasks. With his typical

15

oversensitivity to any sort of adverse criticism, he was too hurt to realize that such insults were more than a sign of the deplorable times, lacking in all respect for those who urged reform from the pulpit; in a sense the crude joke was a measure of his worth, for in a changing world he still represented the dedicated individual for whom the worldly and ignorant had only contempt.

Cotton Mather, with his pride in his name and in his forefathers, with his lifelong attitude of respect for his elders and mentors, with his almost manic bitterness about his detractors or possible detractors, always thought longingly of that earlier New England of religious dedication, of properly revered leaders in her pulpits. The changing New England of his mature years seemed in a sorry way unless she would turn back, be as she had been in the days of the earlier Cottons and Mathers. At the same time that he was regretting the past, he was forming or helping to form a very different New England: one of far more tolerance, of stronger ideals of service to God and man, of progress in science and so in the use of reason. This dichotomy of mind, seemingly unrecognized by himself, made life in many ways difficult for him, especially as he was the victim of a strong if subconscious desire to outrival the great men of the past generations and especially his father.

I *The Diligent Preparation for a Life of Service*

As a young boy raised in a deeply religious Puritan home, Cotton Mather learned early that life was to be taken seriously and that with prayer all difficulties could be faced. Fortunately he was blessed with kind parents, and in time he would base his care of his own children on his father's example. Nevertheless, the youngster was submitted to what would now be considered rigorous training, the more demanding as it was largely self-discipline.

His parents and the Puritan society in which he lived took for granted that at an early age he would assume responsibility for his relationship with his Creator. By the time he was fourteen he was subjecting himself to fasts in order to come nearer to God by disciplining the flesh as he prayed for guidance, a practice that he continued to find useful throughout his life. At sixteen he joined his father's church, confident that he was of the Elect. With his burgeoning sense of duty toward others, he also felt called upon to give religious instruction to his younger brothers and sisters as well as to the family servants.

Scholastically, too, his self-discipline and diligence must have been unsparing as he became proficient in Latin, Greek, and Hebrew before he reached his teens. He was again fortunate in his early schooling. Both his teachers at the Boston Free School, Benjamin Tompson and Ezekiel Cheever, were men of scholarship and distinction who won the heart of their small pupil as they drilled him in grammar and languages and led him through many classical writers, stressing Cicero, Cato, Ovid, and Virgil.

By the time he was twelve, he was well prepared for Harvard. Despite his precocious learning, his first year at college apparently was not very happy, or so the surviving evidence suggests. Not only was he younger than the other students in his class and perhaps a more devoted student than many, but he was the son of the Reverend Increase Mather, at the time (as ruling Fellow) practically running the college. The temptation of his fellow students to haze him, to tease him, to make life miserable for him would indeed be great and quite normal. Adjustment to the new life was not made easier by the fact that at home he had been the eldest, with all the prerogatives that went with masculine seniority; at Cambridge he was but a beginner, with everyone very much his senior.

To make matters worse, the boy stuttered. Not only was this handicap the usual humiliation, but it was also a serious threat to Cotton's hopes of following his father and uncles and grandfathers in their pulpit careers. He was determined, however, even at this early age, to be of use in the world although he might be barred from what the Cottons and Mathers never doubted was the highest form of service. Consequently he turned his thoughts to the possibility of becoming proficient in medicine. By way of preparation he read whatever studies he could find on medical theories and cures, using both his father's library and the college library. This interest in medicine, and in the ways men could be helped to better health (and strength to serve God), remained with him all his life, broadening into his eagerness to take part in the changing contemporary concepts of science.

Neither his early difficulties in adjusting to college nor his devotion of many hours to reading medical lore prevented him from distinguishing himself as a Harvard student, as was to be expected of a young man of his name and background. When he received his Bachelor of Arts degree in 1678, the president of the college effusively predicted that the bearer of two of the most respected names in New England would undoubtedly combine the remarkable abilities of both grandparents, a prophecy that was to comfort Cotton Mather in later years of stress.

Because of his speech difficulty, however, his next step really was very much in question; nevertheless, he continued his theological studies. While he was still debating his future, wanting desperately to preach, a wise man told him that by speaking slowly and deliberately he could overcome his stuttering. His hopes promptly soared. With due prayers for Divine assistance, on occasional Sundays he occupied his grandfather's old pulpit in Dorchester and his father's in Boston. All went well. About this time he built up his confidence in another way, too, for he started to tutor in academic subjects and Hebrew, with his pupils often older than their instructor.

When Cotton Mather proceeded to the Master's degree in 1681, having followed the usual preparatory course for ministers-to-be, no encomiums on his famous name could be delivered as he received his diploma from the hand of his father, then president of Harvard. One of the church offers made to him could not have been unexpected: his father's church, the Second Church (or Old North) of Boston, invited him to assist his father. The struggling church at New Haven also put in a bid for his services. Apparently prodded by this rivalry, the Boston church repeated its offer. The Connecticut call was only to a "small and mean Congregation"; on the other hand, the Boston call obviously meant a place of great prominence in the colonies, with the prospect of large audiences and with the opportunity to be with his respected father. Even so, the young man hesitated rather surprisingly long before deciding definitely to remain in Boston. Without pledging himself, he continued to work as Increase Mather's assistant for some years, father and son serving in the active church and large parish. By 1683 the church decided to ask the younger Mather to be its pastor, as the elder Mather was its teacher. (Many New England churches were thus served by two ministers, with the "teacher" theoretically stressing doctrine and the pastor, faith.) Finally, in May of 1685, Cotton Mather was ordained as his father's colleague.

II   *The Devoted Young Husband and Father*

About the time of his ordination, the young minister, to his naive surprise, found his thoughts turning to the joys of marriage. Soon he was courting Abigail, "the Happy Daughter of John and Katharin

Philips"; he was quickly convinced that God "had reserves of rich and great blessings" in store for him. His marriage to this "lovely and worthy young gentlewoman" took place in the spring of 1686 at her parents' home in Charlestown. The groom was twenty-three, his bride not quite sixteen. For fifteen years he was to know the happiness of marriage with "the Desire of my eyes." His "lovely Consort," as he liked to call the busy Abigail, proved to be the ideal wife, one who was devoted to him and his work, gave him "lovely Off-Spring," and never failed in her tact with his parishioners.

In August of 1687, a little girl was born to the happy couple, named after her mother, and in the fond eyes of her father, "perhaps one of the comeliest infants that have been seen in the world." This first child lived only a brief ten days. Two years later another daughter, Katharine, brightened the little household, and this Katy lived, to study Hebrew and sacred geography, to be an expert needle-woman and a master of penmanship, to show considerable skill in vocal and instrumental music, to study medicine, to read her father's favorite books on German pietism with him—all with proper humility of spirit. But the next two children died, Mary within two years, Joseph after only three days. Then a second Abigail, his Nabby, survived illnesses and such accidents as falling into the fire. The joys of parenthood, however, continued to be marred by "amputations and Resignations." Mehetable lived only a few months; Hannah and Increase, his "only and Lovely" son, grew to maturity, but Samuel died quickly. By the end of 1701 Cotton Mather had had, in his words, five children go home before him—five times he had given His Maker "the Dearest thing on Earth." Four children, all under twelve, were living.

Although he certainly was inclined to think of them in relation to himself, as his possessions, Cotton Mather took genuine pleasure in his children. In his *Diary* he rarely names them without some affectionate adjective or phrase. Each newborn baby is remarkably "lovely" or "comely" or "lusty"—or all three. As his "little Birds" grew they became "my pretty little Nanny," "my lovely Daughter Nibby," "my dear Katy"; when they were ill, their very littleness struck him with anguish. They were gently disciplined, their faults corrected by temporary banishment from their father's presence or by his refusal to teach them something the others were learning, a severe punishment in the father's eyes (and, he believed, in the children's), for the noblest aim in life is to learn, and so be better able to serve God and Man. It is not surprising that in this permissive home the father often resolved that he would have more patience—and that the children should keep better hours, retiring and rising earlier.

On the other hand, as was to be expected, in the Mather home there was no laxity in religious training. The family in health and sickness heard many prayers during the course of a day, for a man who ignored the duty of family prayer was, in Mather's firm words to his congregation, an "atheist and a ostrich, and a more than cruel Sea-monster." The children were catechized from time to time on particular Bible lessons or the last sermon their father or grand-father had delivered. Each meal, too, it was the father's duty and pleasure to tell them an "entertaining" and "useful" biblical story. As soon as they reached an age of understanding, they all learned, through individual prayer-conferences with their father, to consider their religious state: in other words, to live with the idea of death, death that at any hour might come to them or to their father. (Constant indoctrination of this life's being but preparation for the next was not, of course, peculiar to the Mather household, but complete-ly typical of all good Puritan homes.)

III   *Maturity: Its Sorrows and Recompenses*

The early years of the eighteenth century brought Cotton Mather trouble and grief. His much-loved wife, the excellent Abigail, became ill; her prolonged and painful illness lasted nearly a year, with periods of hope that his prayers for her recovery were being answered, inevitably followed by recognition that she was leaving him. She had been sixteen when he married her; as he sadly noted, he had had sixteen years of happiness with her. Finally, on the blackest day of his life, the first of December 1702, she died.

Cotton Mather, always the minister, tried to comfort himself, as he had to do many times in his life, by the thought that he could use his loss to benefit others by his preaching. He very nearly consoled himself in another way not unknown to newly bereaved widowers. An attractive, stylish young lady proposed to him very shortly after Abigail's death. He was sorely tempted by the "poor child," who seems to have had, however, a very doubtful reputation, one that would make her utterly unacceptable to the Second Church. Reluc-tantly, he refused her offer of herself, unwilling to sacrifice his call-ing, and the only result of the episode was a little gossip.

His being in such a vulnerable position, open to attacks by all too desirable young ladies, undoubtedly encouraged Cotton to seek safety in a marriage that would be above the criticism of his parishioners. After one false start, he found a satisfactory answer to his problem in a neighbor, a young widow with one child. In August of 1703 he married Elizabeth (Clark) Hubbard, a daughter of a well-known scholar, Dr. John Clark, and widow of a merchant. If she could not be his first love, the wife of his youth, she was his "dear Consort" and his "dear Friend," a kind stepmother, and soon the mother of a young family of Mathers.

Of the six children of this second marriage, only two lived beyond babyhood. In 1704 Elizabeth was born, her mother's namesake, and in 1706 another Samuel; both of these children lived to maturity, and Samuel survived his father to write the latter's life. But Nathaniel, born in May of 1709, died the following fall. Two years later Jerusha came into the world, to become her father's pet and, by the time she was a one-year-old, his "marvelous, witty, ready, forward Child."

The father's happiness in this second family lasted less than a decade. The blow fell in the fall of 1713. Twin children, Eleazer and Martha, were born at the end of October, during an epidemic of measles. The mother and most of her children and stepchildren became ill, and in less than a fortnight Cotton Mather was again a widower—his "Dear, dear, dear, dear Friend" was dead; he was also bereft of his younger children, Eleazer. Martha, and the much-lamented Jerusha.

IV   *Cotton Mather: The "Man of Sorrows"*

After this sudden, shocking loss of his second wife and her babies, there was little personal happiness for Cotton Mather. Grief from losing members of his family as well as humiliation and threatened humiliation came repeatedly.

The gentle home life that he had had with his first two wives was poor preparation for the hard path he was to travel in his third marriage. With great hopes that he had again found a suitable wife and helpmate, one who would be both a worthy wife of a minister and a kind stepmother to his remaining children, on July 3, 1715, he married Mrs. Lydia (Lee) George, the widowed daughter of Dr. Samuel Lee, a distinguished scholar much admired by the Mathers. The third Mrs. Mather, unfortunately of a very different disposition from her predecessors, proved to be so unstable in her marital relations that Cotton Mather was forced to question her sanity. At times embarrassingly fond of her husband, at other times she left his home (and his fear of public disgrace was great). She insisted on her relatives' joining the family group, and drove at least one of the Mather children from home.

If the years brought some amelioration of these marital difficulties, other sorrows and troubles continued to multiply. Young Increase Mather, the elder of his two surviving sons, was Cotton Mather's one obvious failure in child-rearing; never did a young man fail more completely to live up to his grandfather's illustrious name. Signs of waywardness came early as the boy turned from his prayerful home to gayer company. By the time he was eighteen he was in serious trouble, publicly accused of immorality. The father's efforts could bring him to repentance and back to the family home or to his uncle's home in England, but the reform was always very temporary. Repeatedly the Mather name and position were being threatened by public disgrace.

A near catastrophe of a very different sort also called for Cotton Mather's fortitude and most earnest prayers. This trouble was all the more bitter inasmuch as he had brought it upon himself. Foolishly—he was no business man—in 1717 he acted on his usual impulse to be of service and offered to manage some financial matters for a few of his relatives by marriage. By 1724 he had gotten himself into such monetary difficulties that he was reduced to penury and feared that his beloved library would have to be sold to meet his indebtedness. From this heartbreaking solution (and public shame) he was rescued by some of his parishioners, who raised the necessary money.

The years also steadily reduced the solace and comfort that he, always the affectionate parent, would hope to receive from his maturing family. Of the six children who lived beyond infancy and childhood, four died before their father—all in their twenties. The first of these to go was Katherine; the "dear, good, wise, and lovely Katy," who shared so many of her father's interests, became increasingly ill from tuberculosis, and finally succumbed in December of 1716. Less than five years later the father had to watch Abigail, the Nabby his prayers had saved in repeated childhood accidents and illnesses, die "a long and hard Death" after childbirth. Perhaps the loss by drowning in 1724 of his son Increase, his much-loved, misbehaving young "Cressy," brought both sorrow and relief, but there was added reason for pain as even the fondest father, certain as he was of the salvation of his other children, had to question whether this child was of the Elect and so safe with Christ. Two years later, Elizabeth or Eliza, apparently a very satisfactory daughter, died pathetically as a young matron of twenty-two.

Even as he was bearing these repeated losses, Cotton Mather had to make one other major adjustment in his family relationships and daily life. He had spent his life sharing the responsibilities and duties of the Old North Church with his father, the Reverend Increase Mather, carefully showing him the utmost respect, carefully playing second to him in all church matters, always seeing that the older man had his choice of sermon topics and times. As early as 1716, however, there was talk in the church of the need of a "further supply," that is, a young minister to take Increase's place (if he should become incapacitated or die) or at least to supplement the elderly man's efforts. Gradually the son realized that it was no longer right for him to have only the role of the dutiful, respectful son; he had to become subtly the leader, to manage his father (and the church) so that no untoward difficulties arose. With the death of Increase in 1723, a whole way of life ended for his son. The Reverend Joshua McGee, who had been assisting in the church for some years, became Cotton Mather's colleague, a development that the older minister accepted gracefully, but a change after sharing the pulpit with his father for over forty years.

Often the victim of depression about his health, Mather thought at various times of stress and illness that he was not meant to stay longer in the "uneasy Wilderness" of this world, but the last period of his life, with its sorrows and troubles, not the least of which was his father's prolonged dying with great physical and mental suffering, apparently did hasten his end. During the years after Increase Mather's death, Cotton Mather suffered a number of illnesses, much regretted by him because he could not carry out his pulpit duties or continue his studies. Late in 1727 he felt that his end was approaching, and this time he was correct when he wrote to one of his physicians, "My last Enemy is come, I would say my best Friend." He told watchers by his bedside that he was content, waiting for his will, "the hardest Thing to be killed in me," to be "entirely swallowed up" in the will of God. Samuel Mather, the faithful Sammy who had tried to take the place of the disappointing Cressy in his father's heart, reported that his father was enduring a "hard Cough, and a suffocating Asthma with a Fever"; but at the end it was with "sweet Composure" that Cotton Mather died, on February 13, 1728, one day after his sixty-fifth birthday.

CHAPTER 2

The Busy, Many-Sided
Life of Service

Whatsoever thy Hand finds to do, do it with thy might. (*Ecclesiastes* 9: 10, Cotton Mather's sermon text on his fifty-sixth birthday)

FROM the early 1680s when he started to act as his father's assistant in the Second Church in Boston until his death in 1728, with only brief and reluctantly taken respites due to his own serious illness, Cotton Mather preached from two to five times a week: on Sundays, of course (with his father preaching the other sermon of the day); at least once or twice a month on Lecture-Days, the once-popular midweek gatherings of devout New Englanders to hear another sermon; on fasts (Days of Humiliation) and on Days of Thanksgiving whenever these days of special prayer and rededication were implemented by church of colonial authorities; at funerals; at elections; at many meetings of societies which he had instigated and organized for prayer or Bible study or for the reformation of backsliding Boston. Most frequently, he occupied the Old North pulpit that he shared with his father; but the younger man also made strenuous trips to churches in towns around Boston, and on these visits he was sometimes called upon to preach both morning and afternoon.

Each sermon was carefully prepared, with some days of labor. After his subject and text were determined upon, hours had to be devoted to reading Scripture, endeavoring to obtain the full significance as well as the literal meaning of the text chosen, trying to approach the thought and emotion of the scribe God had chosen to record His will, and seeing the main text and all cited texts in the light of other comparable biblical texts. Many authories on the Bible or on particular books of the Bible had to be used; histories and biographies, hermeneutical commentaries, and spiritual treatises

24

could be consulted. Then the sermon-to-be had to be studied and largely memorized—and, at least ideally, pass the test that the preacher had gained spiritually from it, as he hoped his parishioners would benefit. The whole preparation should be supported by frequent prayers. Indeed, in order to do his duty to his Creator and his congregation, it was Cotton Mather's regular custom to rise from his knees in his study to go to the pulpit.

Other pastoral duties—and these included catechizing, endeavoring to visit all parishioners and faithfully visiting and praying with the sick and bereaved, collecting funds for many good causes, and providing for the needy—could not be neglected, but whatever else he did, directly connected with the church or not, his preaching ranked first in his mind as an honest minister's fundamental obligation. By his sermons he could help men prepare for Grace, and if they were of the Elect to act fittingly, to do good. What could be more important than to show people how to reform themselves, how to derive strength from Christ to bear all their troubles and suffering, how to take comfort in being God's Elect?

In his high endeavor in the pulpit, Cotton Mather evidently did not labor in vain. A good many of his fellow Puritans certainly valued his preaching, regularly filling the Old North Church to hear him; with the years, the church grew steadily, despite some splintering off in 1698 and later in 1721 by dissident groups. It was in recognition of his standing as a Christian leader as well as for his scholarship that the University of Glasgow in 1710 honored him with a doctor of divinity degree. This "civility" from the "most illustrious University in the world" brought ecstatic joy to Cotton, feeling as he did that his own alma mater failed in according him due respect. His father's honorary doctorate from Harvard (conferred before Increase's fall from power in the colony and the college) paled in comparison; so moved was Cotton that for the rest of his life he wore a seal ring with Glasgow's insignia (a tree) to remind him of "the Gravity, the Discretion, the superiour Behaviour, which a *Doctorate* ought alwayes to be attended withal."

Cotton Mather of course did not confine his reading to preparation of sermons and books, however active he was in these allied fields. He read, in Latin, German, and English, all types of books on all subjects. His range of interest was comprehensive: in theology, from the church fathers to German pietism; every book or pamphlet or article on natural science and medicine that he could buy or borrow; in literature, from the classical poets to the moderns of his day, Blackmore and Milton; history, and especially church history. In his maturity he could say that no book reached New England that he did not manage to read, or at least scan for material or ideas new to him.

All his life he had access to his father's extensive library as well as the collections of Harvard College, but he took great pleasure in building up his own library. The acquiring of books always was a major interest with him, one of the important parts of his life; his library came quickly to his mind whenever he felt called upon to list the blessings for which he thanked his Creator. While he never had the opportunities his father had had to haunt London bookstalls during two extended stays in England, the Boston bookdealers (of whom there were as many as twenty by the end of the seventeenth century) imported books, and Cotton Mather dearly loved to guide their selections. Occasionally duplicates from the Harvard library were put up for sale. Books and manuscripts also came to him from the collections of deceased ministers and from friends in the colonies and abroad. With this steady, scholarly accumulation of books and manuscripts he undoubtedly formed the best library in New England, probably in all the colonies, only possibly rivaled by William Byrd's in Virginia.

His frequent preaching, his pastoral duties, his steady preparation of material for the press, not to mention the many, many hours he spent in his library, did not exhaust Cotton Mather's energy. Although he liked to think of himself as longing to devote himself completely to his preaching and scholarship, he obviously was the born crusader, always with a cause. In modern terminology, he was community-minded, very much given to social service of all types. He did not see himself and his church just as a body of men and women united in worship; he not only was cognizant of all the social and political evils in the society in which he lived but he also was certain that he, Cotton Mather, was the one chosen to point out these evils and to correct them.

The needed reforms were many, nor did he limit himself to his own community problems: slave owners, especially in the island and southern colonies, were sinfully remiss about seeing that their Negros became Christians. Many towns in New England lacked schools or really adequate schools; even when there were convenient schools, many parents failed to send their children to them. Conditions in the local jail called for improvement. Ministers in poor towns throughout the colonies were not receiving from their pastorates sufficient funds to support their families. Not only were many positive reforms needed, but many evils should be done away with: the inhuman slave trade, overindulgence in alcohol, houses of prostitution. At least theoretically, Cotton Mather recognized that most reform comes from within the individual, but he was never satisfied with preaching and writing to accomplish his ends if he could also find other means. Usually he tried to influence men in power by personal persuasion and by written appeals; for example, in his attempts to force slave owners to give their slaves the opportunity to become Christians—that is, to see that they had sufficient education to read the Bible or even a catechism—he wrote to prominent officials in the various colonies and tried, through English friends, to have Parliament take the proper steps to make slave owners do their Christian duty.

Cotton Mather also was almost forced into an active interest in political events. This side of a Boston church leader's activities is not surprising since he and every other nonconformist in New England felt that the survival of their churches, perhaps even their own physical survival, depended on the course of events in England and the reflection of these events in the colonies. The last decade and a half of the seventeenth century was a time of great anxiety. The frequent changes in the Crown, the resulting rapid rise and fall of royal favorites and of different political parties, plus the renewal of Catholic versus Protestant shifts in power, made every report from the mother country of vital interest.

The most upsetting development for New England's settlers was the revocation in 1684 of the original charters, the very foundation of the colonies, the assurance that they would have enough independence to maintain their way of life and their churches. With the arrival of a royal governor late in 1686, a decision was reached by Boston leaders that an appeal had to be made directly to the king; the emissaries (of whom Increase Mather was the chief) slipped off to press the colonial cause in London. Then came the news of the Glorious Revolution and the hope for better times, followed by the return of the emissaries in 1692 with a new charter that curtailed the colonists' liberties and forced them to accept governors appointed by the king. Naturally there was dissatisfaction with the new charter, answered by the counterclaims of its advocates that it was the best obtainable. Dramatic, too, was the rise and fall of Sir William Phips, the first governor under the new charter, selected for the position by Increase Mather. These events were not such as could be ignored by the younger leader of Boston's largest and most prominent church, even if his father had not been one of the chief protagonists in the bitter charter controversy.

The young Cotton Mather was not at all averse to taking an active part, to offer his leadership, in the political disputes that accompanied these changes in the colony's status. When the news of the Glorious Revolution crossed the Atlantic in 1689, he cooperated with other men of good will to prevent bloodshed. Very practically, proper leadership was provided for the mobs that descended upon Boston. In 1692 more subtle efforts were needed in the charter difficulties as he labored to convince New Englanders that his father had brought back from England a satisfactory charter, even though the latter was a compromise between the Crown's desire to rule directly in the colonies and the New Englanders' desire to be self-governing (and elect their own governors). In later years (after his father ceased to be president of Harvard and one of the colony's outstanding leaders in politics as well as religion), Cotton Mather could not be as politically active, but he still expressed himself vigorously—usually after he had failed to bring each newly appointed governor into sympathy with Puritan ideas of church polity and colony rule.

Just as Cotton Mather feared for the survival of New England's Puritan churches if the English government and the Crown appointees were hostile to them, so too he feared that, even if the churches were allowed to continue, they would lose their pristine faith without the leadership of men trained in the Puritan tradition of the first ministers, who had been for the most part Oxford and Cambridge men. Early in the colonies' history Harvard College was founded to supply young ministers who would gradually succeed these English-born preachers as church leaders in every town. Therefore Harvard policies and the Harvard curriculum were serious problems decidedly affecting every church in Massachusetts and Connecticut. Cotton Mather did not want the first curriculum blindly adhered to; in fact, he was very critical of part of the college's traditional training. But for him and for men of his way of thinking it was essential that Harvard remain fundamentally a Congregational seminary, controlled by overseers who were Congregationalists (not Church of England men).

When he felt that Harvard College had lost its first sense of purpose (having declined first his father's services and then his own), Cotton Mather turned his hopes to the new college trying to survive in New Haven during the first decades of the eighteenth century. Although he apparently declined to serve as its president, he did more than offer this struggling institution advice and encouragement: he was able to persuade Elihu Yale that his best possible memorial would be to have a college bear his name out of gratitude for his generosity to it.

Thus Cotton Mather, humbly trying to be of service to God and his fellow men, as he would have said (trying to assert himself in every possible way, a true busybody, according to his critics and opponents), managed to fit into his life preaching and church leadership and the many duties of being copastor of a large church, steady preparation of books for the press, constant pursuit of scholarship, leadership in all types of social reform, participation in colonial politics, and the influencing (or attempted influencing) of educational policy.

CHAPTER 3

Man of Religion, Man of Science

TO try to think of Cotton Mather without the faith upon which he built his life is to consider only the husk of the man. His religion (and his position as a religious leader) dominated and controlled him. If this approach to life's problems was not always spontaneous, acceptance came with discipline and application. Throughout his life he conceived of himself as having found the truth in the church of his immediate forefathers and as seeing no reason to swerve from that truth, based as it was on their interpretation of the Bible. Nevertheless, in the forty-five years during which he preached and published so steadily, a natural development and shift in emphasis in his understanding of this precious truth is clearly recognizable; not only was he changing with the times but through his preaching in his large Boston church and his steady stream of publications he was influencing his times.

As a Calvinist he believed (as did all the members of New England's first Puritan churches) in an omnipotent Creator to whom man should be humble and obedient. God's will was to be accepted in all matters and especially in predestination, the determination of who was to be saved, who damned. Man's mind could not equal God's; to try to understand why one man was saved, another—perhaps equally virtuous in the eyes of the casual observer—damned, was to put oneself on the level of God, a grievous sin in itself. According to Calvinist tenets, this division of the Elect and the damned was fair enough, as all men after the fall of Adam were in a state of total depravity or original sin. No one deserved salvation. But God in his great mercy, through the sacrifice of Christ, gave to some men unconditional (everlasting) Election that came from God's Grace. Just as no man in his fallen state had any claim on salvation, no man in his fallen state could possibly earn salvation through merit or works.

Everyone in the Puritan community hoped for some indication

that he was of the Elect, that—after due prayer and preparation—he would have a spiritual experience, an afflatus, that would
make him believe he was so blessed. The danger of this teaching
was fully appreciated: in his great eagerness to be saved, with the
best intent in the world any man could deceive himself, and so
become a self-hypocrite. Then he was indeed a lost soul, inasmuch
as he would not recognize his own condition of sinfulness and
depravity. (And most men of the sincerest faith, including Cotton
Mather, could have times of doubt whether or not they had so
deceived themselves, whether or not they were truly of the Elect.)
Hypocrites in the usual sense of the word, that is, those deliberately
trying to pretend to a state of grace, were a far easier problem and
lived in a less dangerous condition since at any time true faith
might come to them. Nor could any church hope to be free of both
self-hypocrites and deliberate deceivers.

In most New England churches during the seventeenth century
each believer had to tell publicly of the spiritual experience that had
convinced him that he was one of the Elect. The three generations
of Mather preachers—Richard, Increase, and Cotton—put less
emphasis on this regenerative experience than did many of their
fellow New England preachers. It is not surprising, then, that by the
end of the century Cotton Mather had tacitly ceased to stress the
necessity for this positive regenerative experience. (The require-
ment had become a stumbling block for many sincerely religious
members of the congregation.) Instead, he preached from the Old
North pulpit that a man's sincere desire to be of the Elect was the
most hopeful indication that he was indeed one of the Chosen.

Very realistically facing man's weakness (after the Fall), Puritans
recognized that men would sin even after they were in full commu-
nion with God and with their fellow "saints." The Elect could only
repent (publicly if necessary) and try to rise above their evil nature.
God had sacrificed his only Son for them; could they do less than
endeavor to keep Covenant with Him and obey His com-
mandments? The saved could also demonstrate their privileged
state of virtue by doing good works—always keeping the distinction
in mind that virtuous or generous acts could not bring about a
man's salvation (which was not in any sense to be bought). By the
early years of the eighteenth century Cotton Mather's desire to do
good, and perhaps less intensely to have others do good, almost
possessed him. He counted that day lost that he could not devise
some way of doing good: an act of practical charity to the needy,

spiritual assistance to someone, a helpful little book of instruction completed, a large-scale plan for converting whole nations conceived or implemented—the possibilities never ended.

This great devotion to service on Cotton Mather's part can be seen in two lights. It may, of course, be regarded as a form of egoism, the desire to be the most helpful Christian of all, a true disciple. Or it may be seen as an early (and Calvinist) form of eighteenth-century benevolence that put its emphasis on man's behavior to his fellow men and his sincerity in his fundamental Christian beliefs rather than on his doctrinal concepts. In either case, Cotton Mather's devotion to good deeds, his determination to find ways to be of service to his fellow men (and so to God), and his growing ecumenical spirit were strengthened by his reading in conservative German pietism.

Pietism as Cotton Mather admired it in the works of Arndt,[1] Gerhard,[2] Spener,[3] and Francke[4] did not change his ideas or beliefs but confirmed him in his own maturing concept of Puritanism.[5] As he read, he soon recognized that the basic principles of the best tradition of New England Puritanism and of conservative Pietists were much alike; the Pietists, however, had had more success in carrying out these principles to their logical culmination. (The concept of tolerance had indeed been slow in developing in Massachusetts: it was not until well after 1720 that Mather himself had been able to acknowledge that there was truth in Quaker teaching.)

Mather's revered Pietists in their lives and their preaching advocated a return to sincere religion by true reliance on Scripture. In their preaching they stressed man's inner life and that all men of real faith should earnestly try to follow Christ's example in their daily acts. This religion of the heart as well as of the head should lead to brotherly love as expressed in a devoted willingness to help one's neighbor and to be tolerant of this neighbor's differing in minor religious concepts. The success of the Pietist movement in gaining converts, in establishing the University of Halle to inculcate their beliefs, in creating benevolant institutions such as orphanages and schools for the poor, in sending out missionaries, was encouraging to Cotton Mather since it proved to him that men of good will could be recognized for their worth and could accomplish much. Francke's kindly (and respectful) acceptance of him as a fellow laborer spreading the true gospel was a real balm to him, since he always felt that his own New Englanders did not properly honor him for his efforts in their behalf.

The seeds of his own belief in a life of service to his fellow men and in an ecumenical church of all true believers came, however, not from the Pietists but from his lifelong admiration of an old and revered friend of the Mather family, the Reverend Richard Baxter (1615 - 1691), of whom it has been said that he had the one modern mind of all the seventeenth-century English dissenters. By 1650 this Kiddeminster curate, sickly but constantly preaching and publishing, was pointing out that "our Father," a God of infinite love, was the God of all men; therefore men should have a passionate care for Christian unity. Baxter also saw that the close union of body and soul meant that all good men should work to free other men from burdens and temptations—and so find their own joy in helping others. Baxter's gentle influence was felt not only by some men in England and New England, but the works of this visionary reformer were also held in respect by Dutch and German Pietists. In fact, Baxter thus influenced Cotton Mather directly and then through similar Pietist ideas that had absorbed much of Baxter's spirit.

The "Godward orientation of man's soul"—with its concomitant active benevolence and ecumenical spirit—for which Cotton Mather and the Pietists so earnestly strove was not the only influential religious climate of hope shared by many Pietists and Puritans. Cotton Mather believed, as did his father and many of his contemporaries, that the Bible (especially in Revelation 20) foretold a coming Millennium: that is, Christ would rule on earth in a kingdom with his saints for a thousand years before the final Day of Judgment; the colonies were considered a likely site for the New Jerusalem. Before the Millennium a period of deepening corruption would occur, when the Devil would make more violent assaults than usual on God's creation, man. Also before the Millennium the Anti-Christ, the Roman Catholic Church, would have to be destroyed; and the Jews, once God's Chosen, were destined to submit to Christ. Cotton Mather never recanted this interpretation of the Bible, and in his later years he was still preaching on the Second Coming, but with one reservation. In the 1690s many of New England's saints (including the Mathers) thought that their reward would come in the early years of the new century, with varied calculations as to the exact year; when the prophesied years passed, he no longer risked setting or suggesting a definite date.

These chiliastic beliefs explain—or at least throw light up-on—Cotton Mather's thought and actions. Premillenarian assaults by Satan could be the explanation of the outbreak of witchcraft in the 1690s; in other words, the suffering involved and the loss of faith in colonial authorities did not mean only that the colonists were being punished for their sins or general backsliding; the whole devastating experience could also mean that the Millennium was approaching. The almost constant warfare with the Indians also seemed to be of Satanic origin. If this part of the biblical prophecy was becoming apparent, Cotton Mather could see plainly that his duty lay in helping Christendom prepare for its great culmination. For example, his valiant efforts to convert Jews and Spanish Catholics (by instructive manuals) were not chance missionary work, but attempts to bring about the necessary preliminary steps to the Millennium.

The belief in the imminence of the New Jerusalem also gave Cotton Mather a prevailing sense of immediacy, of urgency. If, as he hoped and prayed, he was meant to be a second Calvin completing the great reforms of the first Calvin, if he was meant to be a second John the Baptist preparing the world for the Second Coming of Christ, he had to accomplish as rapidly as possible much in the way of reform and conversion, had to publish his instructive and helpful books as rapidly and frequently as possible. (Pathetically, in his later years, beset by family woes and losses and by his feeling that his efforts to do good went unappreciated, he was inclined to forget these great hopes as he compared himself with Christ—only Jesus had tried harder to serve man; only Jesus had suffered more.)

Cotton Mather had no difficulty in reconciling this concept of himself as a dedicated and supremely useful servant of God with his concept of himself as a natural philosopher. He insisted there was no conflict, and here he was in harmony with the avowed stand of many scientists of his day, including most members of the Royal Society. To him nature and nature's wonders were to be used to demonstrate the Creator's greatness; in fact, science should be "a mighty and wondrous Incentive to Religion." Nevertheless, living in a time of growing dependence on reason (rather than on faith and Bible-teaching) and in a time that man's knowledge of his body and his world was changing rapidly, he could sense that many men would forget the Creator of each newly discovered wonder, whether it was the planetary system or the mechanism of the human eye, in their admiration of the new wonder itself. His purpose, therefore, in writing *The Christian Philosopher* (completed 1715, published 1720), reiterated in every chapter, was to teach men to appreciate—with due gratitude—the wonders of the world that God had created for them; the same theme, somewhat less obviously presented, also pervades his book on medical science, *The Angel of Bethesda* (completed 1724, published 1972).

Despite his deliberate subordination of natural science to religion, Cotton Mather had an active, lifelong interest in the many fields of scientific study that were developing in the seventeenth and eighteenth centuries. As an undergraduate at Harvard he read medical treatises to prepare himself to be a doctor if his stuttering kept him from the ministry, and he retained this interest in reading medical lore all his life. As a young man he presumably took part in the discussions of a shortlived Boston society that his father organized in 1683 as a colonial counterpart of the English Royal Society. By the 1690s he was using his sermons to urge his congregation to become more aware of the wonderful world God had created for them.

Throughout his mature life he was an observer of the natural world around him and an appreciator of other men's observations. Then about 1710 he conceived the idea of being useful (and adding to his prestige) by sending to the Royal Society his own observations on American phenomena as well as other new or surprising bits of information reported to him by his friends and correspondents, for he realized that this august group of scientists and would-be scientists was eagerly seeking to learn more about the New World. There is no doubt that he, fairly tactfully, suggested himself for membership in the society; there also is no doubt about his having been accepted as a member in 1713, although his right to add F.R.S. to his name was nastily denied during the inoculation controversy. Cotton Mather was, in fact, the first American-born colonial member.[6]

Much that this New England member sent over in his frequent letters was not suitable for the Royal Society's purposes since on occasion he "padded" his accounts with excerpts from his reading in the classics and he was not always discriminating in his acceptance and reporting of so-called American phenomena that he heard about. Despite these slips in scholarly acumen, many of his letters were indeed useful: for example, he was the first to report on the hybridization of plants (with different types of corn and with melons and gourds); he advanced the study of botany by his description of six plants not to be found in the herbals of the day; above all, his reports on the successful practice of inoculation in Boston were valuable since they encouraged later workers in this field of preventive medicine.

Although Cotton Mather was extremely proud of his membership in the Royal Society, his attitude that science was the handmaiden of true religion permitted him, without undue harm to his ego, to recognize his position in the burgeoning scientific world. First and foremost, he was a busy colonial minister; he was far removed from English circles where men could experiment, discuss their findings, spark each other to new achievements. For the most part he had to be content to report to the Royal Society phenomena of the New World and, on the other hand, keep his fellow New Englanders informed about discoveries in England and on the Continent. (Only in forcing the issue of inoculating against smallpox did he take an active role of leadership, and here he was intelligently using other men's theories.)

Cotton Mather's growing scientific interest and knowledge of the ordered world about him, with its scientific (and occasionally pseudoscientific) explanations of cause and effect, changed his way of thinking in many ways and so affected both his preaching and his publications. Without his being conscious of the development, he thought of his God more as the great Creator, less as the stern Father demanding absolute, unquestioning obedience and quickly punishing any deviation from the set rules. In other words, with the years Cotton Mather's world became more and more a world of reason—reason, he would have quickly said, that was to be used to support faith. And with reason weighing heavily against dogma, his earlier ecumenical spirit could mature to a more complete understanding of other men and their beliefs.

CHAPTER 4

Service to God and Man
through the Press

What is there that I am further to do, for the Name of God? . . .
I would promote the Publication of a good *Book*, thereby the Souls
of many in the Countrey may be edified. (*Diary*, Vol. I, 88 - 97)

F ROM time to time in his *Diary* Cotton Mather dramatically
accuses himself of sloth. The suspicion promptly arises that this
was a comfortable sin for him to be self-accusatory about, since he
could offer so much evidence of his literary productiveness. Certainly his modern readers may accuse him of various weaknesses, including a pathetic eagerness to appear in print, but no one would
call him indolent by today's standards. He first saw his name on a
title page in 1682, but the items did not start to pour forth until
1689; then the stream was steady to the very year of his death, 1728.
All told, his bibliography[1] consists of 445 printed works, with an additional twenty-four short items, mostly contributions to other
men's works. Many of his publications are short; a number run to a
few hundred pages; a smaller number consist of long, substantial
volumes. (Those starred (°) in this survey are, from the modern
point of view, of sufficient importance and interest to be discussed
in more detail in later chapters.)

Some of his contemporaries openly mocked him for the frequency
of his appearing before them in print. But he persisted, convincing
himself that each production was of service to God and man. This
type of service was by no means alien to him and his ministerial
tradition. His father, Increase Mather, had some 175 items to his
credit. His father's revered friend Richard Baxter, despite constant
poor health, had been able to produce over 160 works that reached
the public. Cotton Mather would have been the last to acknowledge

37

to himself that in any sense he was vying with these respected mentors; he just went on publishing.

How any man constantly preaching, meeting with religious groups, welcoming into his study a good many parishioners and other fellow Bostonians, keeping abreast with both political and scientific developments, could write and usually see through the press so many books remains a never-to-be-solved question. But some light can be thrown on the subject by analyzing his prolific production.

I   Polemic and Instructional Tracts

Certain items in Cotton Mather's long, proudly counted list of publications can be passed over quickly by students mainly interested in Mather as an American writer. With some frequency he wrote tracts on doctrinal disputes and questions of church polity, or in clarification of major Congregational beliefs (the Trinity, the Holy Spirit, Sabbath-keeping, for example). From time to time in his long ministerial career he also composed short manuals on prayer and family worship, copies of which he could leave with his parishioners on pastoral calls. He also wrote and had printed short catechisms of various types, intended to help children, Indians, and Negroes. Another type of instructive book. one of his favorites, gathered together tales of early piety.

II   Sermon Literature

Considered numerically, at least two-thirds of Cotton Mather's publications are sermons,[2] printed much as they had been heard by his parishioners (but frequently carrying added apropos facts, biographical or historical). Over 275 titles in his bibliography represent his preaching, each book containing from one to eight discourses. Most frequently one or two sermons form slender little books (with soft covers) that seem like pamphlets, usually of not more than twenty-odd to fifty pages.

Although only a fraction of his pulpit oratory of more than forty-five years of steady pulpit service, his printed sermons show his (and New England's) development through the years and what he (and presumably his congregation) considered of importance in religious and social ideas. A number of the sermons are autobiographical and biographical: deaths in his own family and the congregation called for sermons. More frequently, his own (or his parishioners') emotional difficulties are apparent as he talks of fear during an economic depression, the problem of debt, the duties of children to parents, of parents to children, or the dangers of various heresies that seemed to be corrupting or trying to corrupt the faithful. No matter what his ostensible topic, his listeners and then his readers were instructed (or reinstructed) about such fundamental tenets as the Covenant between man and God, the doctrine of the Elect, Predestination, the temptations of the Devil, the need for prayer and repentance, the joys of Salvation and Heaven. They were also urged to be loyal to their church, to be strict in their Sabbath-keeping, to show their faith through good works, to be honest, to avoid covetousness, to increase their missionary zeal, and to be tolerant.

Sometimes friends, singly or in groups, paid for these frequent printings; sometimes sincere and impressed parishioners defrayed the costs; one time a member of the congregation was overcome by drowsiness during the services and then apologized (and saved his soul or at least his standing in the community) by paying for the sermon's printing so that many could benefit by Mather's golden words; often relatives made arrangements for funeral sermons to be preserved in print. On rare occasions, Mather himself paid, declaring that the message in question would be of essential help to his erring contemporaries.

However the publication was managed, quickly and easily or only after considerable maneuvering on his part, the preacher at times had the satisfaction of having his labors (and prayers) meet with quick success, with as many as a thousand copies being sold in a week. But at times his sermons, as well as his other instructive tracts, found their audience in less-flattering ways, for he often distributed a good part of an issue through his pastoral calls; occasionally he arranged for distribution through other churches. But one way or another, his preaching and instruction obviously reached many of his fellow New Englanders.

The life of some of these slim, paperbound sermons was somewhat ephemeral, however, since even in his own day a number of them, apparently worn out by having been read and reread, had completely disappeared. On the other hand, he frequently gave new life to his sermons by incorporating them into his longer works: the *Magnalia Christi Americana,*° *Bonifacius,*°and *The Angel of Bethesda*° all contain sermons that have undergone little or no alteration from their pulpit form. Sometimes, too, Cotton Mather's preaching survived even though it had lost its first form. The frequent short tracts that he wrote on religious, social, political, and economic issues undoubtedly echoed earlier arguments and pleas that he had made from the pulpit for New England to change her sinning ways.

III   *Biographies and Histories*

Closely connected with the funeral sermons that he was so often called upon to deliver is another type of literary work, one in which Mather showed considerable skill. During his life he wrote close to 200 biographies. Some of these, the shorter ones, were appended to funeral sermons; for example, in 1705 he attached "Some observable & Serviceable Passages" to a sermon delivered at the death of Reverend Michael Wigglesworth, a minister and poet best known for his very Calvinistic *The Day of Doom* (1662). Three years later, in a sermon entitled *Corderius Americanus*, Mather paid similar tribute to his old schoolmaster, the Latin scholar Ezekiel Cheever, and in so doing told much about Boston schooling in the second half of the preceding century. Other biographies of greater length appeared separately or in small collections; for example, in 1695 Mather presented the public with *Johannes in Eremo*, the lives of four well-known divines of the first generation to occupy New England's pulpits, all with the first name of John—John Cotton, John Norton, John Wilson, and John Davenport—and then for good measure added an account of the Reverend Thomas Hooker. As can be seen by his choice of subjects, Mather often thought it his duty to write about the Congregational clergy of his own and previous generations.

But the virtues of the ministry formed only part of his biographical output. He also recorded the careers of laymen of prominence in colonial affairs, especially if they had been among his parishioners or friends. The best-known of these secular lives is his *Pietas in Patriam: The Life of His Excellency Sir William Phips, Knt.* (1697), a more detailed account than he usually attempted. Inasmuch as the late governor had acquired the usual friends and enemies during his tenure in political office, the book met with a mixed reception. Its author has been accused, both in his own time and later, of prejudice in favor of Phips, an obvious charge as the latter had been Increase Mather's choice for governor under the new charter. One-sided though it may be, the biography has vitality and manages to indicate convincingly the type of adventurous sea captain that Phips was.[3]

Many of the lives written before 1700, including those in the *Johannes in Eremo* collection and Governor Phips's biography, were used again by Mather as part of the longer work he was preparing at this time, his *Magnalia Christi Americana°* (1702). The inclusion of earlier biographies in this major opus is paralleled by his similar use in the *Magnalia* of earlier historical accounts, another type of publication that was closely connected with his pulpit work. Just as Mather frequently combined a biography with a funeral sermon, so he was also given to supplying short historical accounts to appear with appropriate sermons. For example, in *The Boston Ebenezer* (1698) he rapidly surveys Boston's past and then prints a lengthy sermon on the city's current sins. But his longer histories have sufficient body to stand by themseves, and any sermon printed with them appears to be attached to the main historical work. Perhaps the most successful of these more ambitious accounts is his *Decennium Luctuosum* (1699), a still-standard history of the Indian wars from 1688 to 1698. Despite its minor errors, modern historians have found this history of a complicated period of colonial strife not only the most useful one available but also genuinely readable and interesting.[4]

IV *Major Works*

Not content with the service he was rendering to his fellow men by all these shorter publications (or perhaps not satisfied that the latter were establishing him as a scholar of note), Cotton Mather early determined to set himself projects on a much grander scale. In 1693 he started to collect material for three lengthy works that obviously would involve considerable scholarship. These undertakings were to be carried on at the same time, and they were not to interrupt his steady production of less useful publications, nor were they to interfere with his pastoral obligations.[5]

Of the three projects, the previously mentioned *Magnalia Christi Americana°* was actually published during the author's lifetime. This combination of biography and history was Mather's attempt to keep men in a rapidly changing New England from forgetting the religious dedication·that had characterized the first generations of settlers. For the other two major undertakings, despite the hours devoted to them for many years and then very persistent attempts to get them into print, the author never could arrange publication, much to his distress. (The ponderous size of these manuscripts did much to make publication very difficult.) The *Biblia Americana*, a Bible commentary to which Mather was adding points as late as 1713, still lies in its six large volumes of manuscript.[6] *The Angel of Bethesda*,° intended to instruct men concerning the rules of health and to give all available knowledge about diseases (and the religious lessons to be learned from them), met a kinder fate, but for the most part posthumously. Although one chapter was printed in New London in 1722, a complete edition did not appear until 1972.

In addition to these three lengthy testimonies to his diligence and scholarship, Cotton Mather during the last twenty years of his life wrote three shorter books of importance. The first of these has been much reprinted and is the most obviously influential of all his many volumes: *Bonifacius: An Essay upon the Good that is to be Devised and Designed by Those Who Desire . . . to do Good*° (1710) is succinct, practical advice for all classes of people on how they can improve themselves and their community. The second, *The Christian Philosopher*,° finished in 1715 but not published until 1721, is Mather's attempt to reconcile religion and the new science, a philosophical difficulty that thoughtful men of the age, especially Mather's fellow members of the Royal Society, were necessarily exploring. *The Christian Philosopher*, despite the difficulties of its subject, is a book of only three hundred - odd pages. The *Manuductio ad Ministerium, Directions for a Candidate of the Ministry*,° published in 1726 and Mather's last important book is much shorter, but again covers an extensive subject: the education, both practical and scholastic, of a New England minister planning to manage his congregation even as he led them to God.

V   *Private Writing*

In addition to these tracts, sermons, biographies, and histories that were the work of a week or two or of some months, and the major works that often involved many years of work (and really were the fruits of a lifetime of reading), Cotton Mather wrote much that he did not try to publish, although he was not always averse to having it find readers. Such more or less private products of his desk fall into a number of categories.

Whether a man lived in England or New England during the

seventeenth and eighteenth centuries, one essential way for him to keep in touch with a changing world was through correspondence. Cotton Mather exchanged letters[7] with ministers and other men of prominence in both the continental and island colonies. In other words, he had a fair idea of church and political events in New York, Long Island, New Jersey, Pennsylvania, Virginia, Carolina, Barbados, Antigua, Nevis, St. Christopher's, Montserrat, Bermuda, and Jamaica. He also took great pride in his "ultramarine" correspondents. These included the Dutch scholar and theologian Dr. Herman Witsius (1636 - 1708) and the noted English mathematician and theologian William Whiston (1667 - 1752). Among contempoary English writers of some note, he was on friendly terms with Sir Richard Blackmore (c. 1650 - 1729), one of the most prominent poets of his day; daniel Defoe (1661 - 1751), then noted as a pamphleteer rather than as a novelist; and Isaac Watts (1674 - 1748), now remembered as a writer of hymns but much respected in his own day for his numerous prose works on religious subjects. During his mature years of prominence and activity Mather often wrote annually as many as fifty long, carefully letters of facts and ideas that he felt would be of interest to other intellectual and religious leaders; he complained of the labor involved, but the very complaints plainly show his pride in his distinguished correspondents.

In Mather's later years he also added the burden of collecting from correspondents and from his own reading whatever he thought would interest two distinct sets of men: members of the Royal Society and the dominant leaders in German pietism. The latter movement was devoted to educational reform and missionary work, and Mather's letters to his German friends reflect these purposes. On the other hand, the eighty-odd letters to the Royal Society, his *Curiosa Americana°* (1712 - 1724), have particular importance since they show their author's desire to be part of the new interest in seeking scientific knowledge by observation of natural phenomena. Some of these accounts that Mather as a dweller in America sent "home" to England were *in toto* or in excerpts by the society, an honor that their reporter certainly appreciated. More of these letters remained in manuscript, to be passed around among members of the society.

Except for his letters to the Royal Society, his correspondence with other clergymen and scholars naturally was written without a constant eye on the possibilities of publication. His yearly *Diaries°*

also were not intended for the printer, although these annals were not meant to go completely unread. Mather hoped that his children (and perhaps other readers as well) would benefit from his recording of his spiritual life and his daily efforts to do good. These *Diaries*, with their frequently very personal revelations about their writer, have been published, while his *Paterna*,[8] an autobiography based on the *Diaries* but much shorter (and less intimate in tone), has remained in manuscript, along with a number of his other literary efforts that he yearned to see in print.

Cotton Mather's letter-writing and diary-keeping were lifelong occupations. At one time, briefly, the Boston minister tried his hand at another type of literature not intended for publication but decidedly meant to have readers. In defense of his father's integrity and acumen in securing the compromise charter of 1689, the younger Mather wrote a series of simple and obvious allegories that circulated in manuscript. Although these brief fabes show more creative ability than anything else their author wrote, they did not find their way into print until the nineteenth century.[9]

Mather also wrote much that he really did not intend for any eyes but his own. These private writings—commonplace books, sermon notes, and various lesser records—have some interest in themselves as records of influences on their writer, but they are also valuable evidence of how naturally Cotton Mather, like any other educated man of his day, almost automatically organized and clarified his ideas by written expression of them.

Following the practice of many men of the period, including Locke and Newton, he kept a commonplace book, or really a series of such books. He called them his Quotidiana.[10] As he read, he copied into a handy blank book particularly important or effective passages. Thus he could perserve for himself in convenient form whatever pieces of information or inspirational passages he considered of value. Then, too, he could record his judgment of the many authors he read; for example, upon reading Dryden's translation of Virgil, he jotted down that it was fair, but no version in a modern language could equal the original. Like other ministers and writers, Mather also used his commonplace books as storehouses of illustrations to be drawn upon to strengthen a point by apt citing.

As did many other men in an age that had a genuine interest in pulpit oratory and considered seriously every point made by the preacher, Cotton Mather kept notes on sermons he heard, whether delivered by his father in the regular course of his preaching or by neighboring or visiting ministers on Lecture-Days and special occasions; some twenty-six little books of such recordings survive.[11] At one time he dropped the habit because he realized that he was doing quite a bit of writing. Then when he found that he was profiting less from the sermons he heard, he resumed the practice, although in later years he did not always bother to put down the lesson to be learned from each discourse.

VI   *Verse*

It is obvious from this rapid survey of his main types of printed and unprinted work that Cotton Mather usually expressed himself in prose; certainly he is remembered not as a poet or even a verse-maker but as a prolific writer of prose. Nevertheless, like most of his educated contemporaries, he was a capable (if not inspired) writer and translator of poetry.

Even without his major nonprose work, his *Psalterium Americanum,* his collected verse would make a respectable little volume. Although his poetical efforts are always devotedly religious, his work can be divided into four categories, with the poems in the first category seeming to show a pleasing spontaneity. Inserted in many of his longer works, including his *Diary,*° the *Magnalia Christi Americana,*° and some of his shorter publications, are brief (or fairly brief) emotional ejaculations or hymns of praise to his Maker; these run in length from couplets to thirty-odd lines. More labored and of greater body, sometimes appearing as separate publications, are his elegies and epitaphs for departed relatives and friends. These tributes he usually wrote in English, but occasionally—as a mark of great respect—he composed them in Latin. His third type of versifying was definitely practical as he rhymed important key passages in the Bible, such as the Lord's Prayer, so that young children could memorize them more readily. Utilitarian, too, but on a higher level and surely a decided pleasure for him, was his turning into rhymed couplets a number of Psalms and other passages in the Bible so that they could be sung more easily by congregations.[12]

In his later years Mather still saw the value of preparing the Psalms for congregational singing. But now he saw the penalties of using rhyme in translating: the necessity of the rhyme might force the exclusion of valuable points or it might encourage the insertion of extraneous words or phrases. He felt that his *Psalterium*

Americanum. The Book of Psalms, . . . All in Blank Verse (1718) was free from such errors and met the all-important criterion of being as close as possible to the Hebrew. (This translation is the first extensive use of unrhymed verse in New England.)

Cotton Mather indeed could safely consider the question of his possible sloth. Even when the multiple use he often made of his material is recognized, his output is prodigious. The very quantity of his work as well as its variety is so staggering that a modern reader may forget this labor had one avowed purpose: to be of benefit to all earnest men trying to find the right road to God. In believing that this noble aim was the only reason for all his efforts, Cotton Mather all too apparently was deceiving himself, as his *Diary* pathetically shows. His agony over a lost manuscript or a destroyed leaf in one of his diaries, his gnawing worry that some piece of work was not finding quick printing, his exultation at the appearance of each book or pamphlet, his childish joy in counting his publications, all indicate the tremendous satisfaction that he enjoyed from being so "fruitful." As he wrote in one of his devastating moments of honesty with himself, "*Proud Thoughts* fly-blow my best performances!"

CHAPTER 5

Diary

Good Resolved for Saturday mornings: "That I would sometimes insist on that Enquiry, *what do I that no Hypocrite ever did?*" (Vol. II, 29)

T HE habit of keeping a diary was indeed common in the seventeenth and eighteenth centuries, at least among literate (and sometimes semiliterate) men. It was very natural for Cotton Mather to devote some of his crowded day to his diary, as his grandfathers had done and as his father and his own contemporaries, including Samuel Sewall, were doing. But, being Cotton Mather, he created a diary that varies in a number of ways from most run-of-the-mill daily accounts.

Taken together, his yearly journals form a substantial piece of work[1] that he started at least as early as his eighteenth year and presumably continued to almost the end of his life, although the last years are missing, as are many of the intervening years. (The preserved volumes start with 1681 and end with the first months of 1725; of these forty-three years, only twenty-six have survived.) It is worth noting that for him all years started with his birthday, February 12, and he saw no evidence of his loathed sin of pride in this automatic decision.

He did not mean the diary to be for his eyes alone; on the contrary, he hoped that his children, and perhaps others as well with whom he might leave his papers, would benefit from reading it (Vol. I, 11). Significantly, his own title for the earlier volumes was "Revised Memorials," suggesting not only his conscious intent that these records should be respectfully kept and perused but also that he had not been content to leave each day's notes unimproved. As a matter of fact, he did not hesitate to elaborate upon an occasional passage, making marginal comments when he reread, and inserting afterthoughts or later proofs of some point. So a sacrifice made for his father's comfort would get its just reward years later, with the happy outcome recorded in the proper place, the time of the sacrifice.

One careful habit Mather cultivated throughout the diary: when an event or discovery was too sacred or too painful to be read by an unknown child or friend or member of his household, he clothed the revelation in Latin or Greek, presumably thinking to limit future readers of these passages to his son or sons who would follow him in the ministerial paths of learning. Accordingly, when his good angel appeared in his study to comfort him and to assure him that his prayers would be granted, no ignorant reader would mock the sincerely believed-in ecstatic experience; on the sorrowful side, his discovery of his passionate third wife's mental condition was such a painful blow that it had to be obscured from the vulgar eye. More than occasionally, too, with some delicacy he translated into Greek the names of those receiving his charity.

The youthful Cotton Mather had no intention of recording the daily events of his life or interesting happenings in colonial Boston, as his friend Samuel Sewall was doing.[2] The records of the early years consequently avoid both the details of life and current events. A man's spiritual growth was far more important than mundane affairs, and the young man obviously was very fond of introspection.

In the first years of his ministry he self-consciously considered his sins and made lists of resolutions for his improvement. He was also given to listing his blessings. In 1683, when he was twenty, not only was he thankful for such "spiritual Blessings" as his faith and confidence in his salvation, but he had received "further Favours of God":

1.   My Improvement in the *Ministry* of the Gospel, after I have been the vilest Creature in the World.
2.   The many *Advantages*, which I have to countenance mee, in that Improvement.
   1.   The miraculous Freedome of my *Speech*. [He had cured his speech impediment.]
   2.   A *Library*, exceeding any man's, in all this Land.
   3.   A desireable *Acceptance*, among the People of God.
   4.   An happy *Success* of my Labours, both public and private, upon Hundreds of Souls (Vol. I, 77).

Two years later, in 1685, he has much the same list of God's kindnesses to him, but this time he decides to repay his Maker by renewed diligence in performing a time-consuming duty:

This day, I sett apart for *secret Thanksgivings* before the Lord.

In the former Part of the Day, I sang, I read, I thought, and on my Knees, I mentioned, such occasions to *speak well of God,* as I had heretofore took Notice of.

In the Afternoon, I thanked the Lord,

1. For His gracious Works on my *Heart.*
2. For my *Improvement* in the *Ministry* of His Gospel.
3. For my *Acceptance* among His People.
4. For the *Success* of my Labours, become very manifold and visible.
5. For my *free Utterance.*
6. For my *large Library.*

And in Thankfulness to the Lord, I invigorated my Design to *visit the Families of the Flock* (Vol. I, 102 - 103).

In the following years he could add his thankfulness for being given the strength to resist (unnamed) temptations and for his sorrows that had taught him acceptance and brought him closer to God. He is also grateful for his Boston pulpit with its possibilities of large audiences and for the colonial printing presses that enabled him to reach many more.

But after 1700 the listing ceases; there is too much else to record. More and more he discovered that his spiritual life could not be separated from the emotions of his daily life. It is the middle years of the diary that come closest to being Cotton Mather's autobiography. As a man who came from a large family and who in turn had three wives and fifteen children, as a church leader whose interest in preserving his church involved participation in both educational and political issues, as New England's foremost preacher and producer of books, he went from one crisis to another that needed days of fasting and prayer. And if he no longer listed his blessings, he fervently gave thanks for each ill child's survival—alas, often very temporary—for each victory for the right (his) side in every dispute, and for all his opportunities to serve the Lord by particularly effective preaching or by more and more books gotten through the press. But the tale as a whole is far from a happy one: there were few lessons in the acceptance of God's will that Cotton Mather did not learn, although sometimes only after complete despair and loss of faith.

As early as 1705 Mather recognized his keen pleasure in acts of mercy and kindness. He happily notes charity given to the suffering poor during a very cold December, a scheme for charity schools, plans for converting Negroes and Indians, his advocacy of the settlement of Scots colonies to the north of Massachusetts. By 1708, after a period of despair, he found he had "a flaming Zeal, to do good, abundantly" (Vol. II, 3). By 1710, one "Good Devised," shortened to "G.D.," follows another; as he notes in 1713, "The grand intention of my life is, *to do Good*" (Vol. II, 263). During the last weary years he forces out of his flagging energy one short "G.D." for each day of the month.

As the "G.D.s" take over the diary, the earlier chronological coherence is lost, and all semblance of order and development disappears. Mather's ways of helping his fellow men ranged from the homely to the grandiose, from seventeenth-century religious fervor to eighteenth-century practicality.

Some of his proposed services are happily definite and immediately practicable. A widow is to be invited to dinner. (Boston seems to have had an endless supply of hungry widows who must have felt honored to dine at their pastor's table.) He will put up instructive mottoes in every room in his house, to help himself and his children remember their duty. His daughters' penmanship needs improvement. In this next letter to Defoe he will suggest that the latter write a history of the persecution of Dissenters by the Church of England. He will always have pennies or paints or fruit with him for the children he meets on the streets or in his pastoral visiting.

But some of his helpful ideas are less easily carried out. Formality among church members must be avoided, and the old sincerity of faith returned to. Neighborliness must be encouraged. He endeavors to have Boston's houses of prostitution closed. A good minister willing to go to Bermuda has to be found. An evening school for Negroes and Indians should be established. The French, Spanish, and Jews are to be converted.

Occasionally he recognizes that he cannot do the whole job himself, even though he gives from his own purse, learns Spanish (in five weeks) to convert the Catholics in the West Indies, preaches two-hour sermons four and five times a week, and repeatedly produces instructive books of all types. In such pragmatic moments he arranges for rich orphans to help poor orphans, for people who have come into sudden prosperity by a fortunate shipping venture to express their thankfulness by charity, for two old people to marry and so combine their meager incomes, for the governor of New York to see that the Indians on Long Island are under proper Christian influences. And, as if a little regretful that he has had to allow others to share his good intentions, he prays that he will appreciate the good deeds of other people.

The individual projects that fill the last years of the *Diary* often are of great interest not only for their revealment of Cotton Mather's mind but also for the light they throw upon many facets of colonial life in the first quarter of the eighteenth century. Nevertheless, the rapid juxtaposition of such divergent ideas one upon another is inclined to weary the reader, who usually knows neither the individual recipients of specific good deeds nor the degree of success achieved by the author's plans of a larger scope.

It should also be said that the *Diary* as a whole has other stumbling blocks to the modern reader's enjoyment of it. As in all accounts that cover many years, there is a certain amount of understandable repetition. Births, illnesses, deaths, preaching to large audiences, trips to neighboring pulpits, books prepared for the press and anxieties about their publication—all these are recorded many times, as are his many, many days of private fasting and prayer.

Sometimes, too, this repetition is accompanied by set terminology that now seems painfully artificial. Calvinists were inclined to bewail their vileness, and Cotton Mather was no exception as he notes his sinfulness and unworthiness of God's favor. To this general habit of speaking of man's weakness in terms that later generations have found somewhat ridiculously self-derogatory, Mather added a sense of the dramatic. So when he pleads with the Lord, the tableau is always the same:

Being prostrate, in the Dust on my Study-floor, after many Fears of a sad, heavy, woful Heart, that the Holy Spirit of the Lord Jesus Christ, grieved by my Miscarriages, would forsake mee utterly, that Spirit of the Lord made an inexpressible Descent upon mee. A Stream of Tears gushed out of my Eyes, upon my Floor, while I had my Soul inexpressibly irradiated with Assurances, of especially two or three Things, bore in upon mee (Vol. I, 187).

Two weeks later such as "the treacherous Wickedness" of his heart and his "extraordinary Vileness" that he again fasts and

Afterwards prostrate on my Study-floor, when I was representing before the Lord, that I was employ'd in *great Work* for Him, . . . my Heart was after an astonishing Manner, melted before the Lord, with a strange Assurance, which I received, even as if it had been spoken from Heaven unto mee. . . . In the uttering of which Assurance, my Tears ran down upon my Study-floor, with *Joy unspeakable and full of Glory* (Vol. I, 193).

If such descriptions of his religious throes seem remarkably

stereotyped, at other times the diarist unconsciously reveals himself
so completely that he becomes a complex, interesting human being.
The pompous preacher as seen in many of his publications, always
trying to tell others what to believe and think and do, disappears as
one reads of the very different relationships he had with his three
wives and the additional young lady who yearned (and demanded)
to be his wife: young love (with his first wife); widower, flattered
and tempted (by an ardent admirer who would not be acceptable to
his congregation); marital friendship (with his second wife); and
late sex passion (with his unfortunate, unstable third wife).

Not only as a husband and lover but also as a father he found that
life could be difficult and painful as he endured bereavement after
bereavement. The children may have been many and the father
busy, but there was a special tenderness and tie with the oldest
daughter surviving babyhood, his dear Katy, who in the last years of
her short life shared his enthusiastic reading of the German Pietists.
Dutiful Samuel, after getting over a nasty desire in childhood to
play, was all a son should be as he followed in his father's
ministerial footsteps, but it was beloved, sinful Cressy, wandering at
night from his father's prayerful house, who broke his father's heart
long before the young man's death by drowning. If the failure of his
parental efforts and prayers with this one wayward child was a long
heartache (and obvious embarrassment), sorrow of another nature
came to him frequently as death took his young children. The fond
father wrestled with the Lord for the life of each sick child, but
could send the loved little one confidently before him to heaven;
and then came Jerusha, that most remarkably beautiful and intelligent baby girl, to teach him new lessons in acceptance when he
buried her before her third birthday.

Although Cotton Mather's interrelations with his wives and
children necessarily loom large in the *Diary*, there is much more of
his life to be found in its pages. Understandably, in none of his
other works did he permit so much that was personal to appear: his
changing attitude toward his father (from a youngster's profound
admiration, to a fellow minister's respectful collaboration in the
work of the North Church, to a sympathetic son's cautious protection of an aging parent whose wisdom in church and political crises
was decidedly open to question); his emotion about a dying sister
who had suffered from an unfortunate marriage; his reaction to
prosperity and to poverty; his successes in preaching and in

publishing; his hurt pride in his failure to follow his father in the presidency of Harvard; his alternate elation and distress as he and his father were in and out of favor with different colonial governors; his joy in the size of his congregation but his recognition that new churches should be formed for the convenience of Boston's growing population. In fact, so near does the *Diary* come to giving the many sides of its writer that Barrett Wendell was able to base on it whole sections of his very readable book[3] on Cotton Mather, regularly using the wording of the original journal.

Granted that its revelation of its author's personality and approach to life is the main purpose for reading the *Diary*, its pages are also brightened by an occasional passage that stands out from the steady day-by-day journal or the "Good Devised" listing. Sometimes the reader smiles at homely sentiment vividly worded:

> Alas, for a very great Part of my time, I am *dead*. It is consumed in *Sleep*. Thro' my *Feebleness*, and, I doubt, I may more truly say, thro my *Slothfulness*, I sweel away the precious Morning. I rise not until *seven* or *eight* a Clock (Vol. I, 545).

Or a bit of description brings someone alive:

> G.D. I have a Neighbour, my next Neighbour, who is a very froward, frappish, peevish Creature; and who in his ungoverned Passion committs many Offences; He is an Aged Professor of Religion. I must therefore, as lovingly, as winningly, as prudently and faithfully as I can, take him into my Hands, and labour to recover him out of a Distemper, which renders him uneasy unto himself, and unto all about him (Vol. II, 135 - 36).

Sometimes, too, Mather makes his points effective by the apt use of metaphor:

> G.D. *The Snuffing of my Candle* is a very frequent Action with me. I have provided a great Number of Pertinent *Thoughts*, and *Wishes*, and *Prayers* and *Praises*, to be form'd upon the Occurrences in my Life, which afford Occasions for them. I have not yett made so particular a Provision for this, as I now do. In the Doing of this Action, I would often think, and wish, and say, *Lord, Lett me shine the brighter, for all my afflictive Diminutions!* (Vol. II, 281)

Although his health failed him in his last years, he could still make his point effectively, pathetically:

I had three Maladies now [November 1724] to conflict withal. A *Cough*
which proved a grievous Breast-beater; an *Asthma* which often almost suf-
focated me; and a *Fever*, which held me every Afternoon. . . . Particularly, I imposed it as a Rule for me, that whenever any Fitt of my tedious and
irksome Coughing should come upon me, I would strive to have some new
Thoughts of the blessed JESUS raised in me. And I was gloriously supported by the Comforter who releeved my Soul, and caused me to triumph
over the Fear of Death, and enabled me to sing the Songs of the Lord in a
strange Land, and entertain my Visitors with such Flights to the Heavenly
World, and Views of it, and News from it, as, I hope, honoured Him, and
had a great Impression upon them.

After five weeks of Confinement, the God of my Life returns me to my
Study, and to a prospect of serving Him again in the Public Sacrifices (Vol.
II, 775).

Such passages, in varying degrees effective and pathetic,
sometimes unconsciously amusing, are to be found sporadically
throughout the *Diary*. And at least once, under the stress of his first
great sorrow, he was able to share his emotion with his readers in
one of the most moving scenes in colonial literature. His beloved
first wife, whom he had married when she was sixteen and with
whom he had had sixteen happy years, was dying. He had been
convinced that she would live; time and time again he had fasted
and prayed for her recovery and felt certain—had a "particular
faith"—that she would be spared to him. But now he had to admit
that she was going. Perhaps the Lord had been trying merely to
soften the blow by reassuring him as she lingered. Nevertheless, her
approaching death was a double blow: he, Cotton Mather, doing
God's work, with his own angel to reassure him when necessary,
could no longer be sure of the answers to his prayers since he had
been so completely mistaken; and, with "this terrible Death" of his
"Prayer and Faith," he was losing the love of his youth, the mother
of his young children, the ideal "minister's wife" who had assisted
him in countless ways. Then, on that last "black day," his strength
returned to him:

So, two Hours before my lovely Consort expired, I kneeled by her Bed-
Side, and I took into my two Hands, a dear Hand, the dearest in the World.
With her then in my Hands, I solemnly and sincerely gave her up unto the
Lord; and in token of my real RESIGNATION, I gently putt her out of my
Hands, and laid away a most lovely Hand, resolving that I would never
touch it any more!

This was the hardest and perhaps the bravest Action, that ever I did. She afterwards told me, *that she sign'd and seal'd my Act of Resignation.* And tho' before that, she call'd for me, continually; she after this never asked for me any more (Vol. I, 448 - 49).

CHAPTER 6

Witchcraft: Cotton Mather's Part in the "Sad Errours" of 1692

MOST young students—and a good many older ones brought up in the same hazy tradition—think of the witchcraft cases in colonial New England as nasty but interesting tragedies peculiar to the Puritan ethos. If Cotton Mather's name is known at all, it is as the odd name of some one responsible for the whole occurrence. Both suppositions are quite wrong, and eventually our American elementary and high schools textbooks will catch up with the truth.

In the long history of superstition and the resulting cruelty of man to man, the outbreak of witchcraft that centered around Salem Village (now Danvers) in 1692 is a minor chapter. True, some twenty people were put to death and some three hundred others were involved in various accusations that suddenly became common as old neighbor testified against old neighbor, brother against sister, husband against wife, child against mother, pastor against parishioner as well as parishioner against pastor. The tale is a pathetic one, with much heartache involved, but it was only one episode in a series of similar crises of fear that marked European Christianity for many generations.[1]

The belief in Satan's strength and man's weakness had been so rife in European countries during the fifteenth and sixteenth centuries that tens of thousands if not hundreds of thousands had been put to death for the supposed sin of entering into a contract with the Devil to do his bidding. Nor had the periodic local intensifications of fear and incrimination in both Catholic and Protestant countries ceased during the seventeenth century. As late as the winter of 1669 - 1670, for example, there had been a serious eruption of charges and countercharges in Sweden with hundreds of men, women, and children involved, followed by the legal execution of some seventy judged guilty.

Notwithstanding this European history of witchcraft epidemics, certain American social historians of the nineteenth century showed a decided tendency to consider the Salem catastrophe as a separate phenomenon peculiar to its time and place, an ironic example of the innate cruelty and completely prejudiced minds of men who pretended to be God's Elect. Another blatantly anti-Puritan assertion, based on extremely haphazard and twisted evidence, was made more than occasionally: the Mathers, Increase and Cotton, but especially the son Cotton, were charged with stirring up the whole trouble for some unnamed profit or addition to their power.[2] Despite the efforts of more responsible historians[3] to record the whole series of events, to determine causes as far as they could be ascertained, and to take into consideration all that the Mathers actually wrote and did during the crucial period, the accusations have lingered with unfortunate perversity. Cotton Mather and witchcraft are all too often linked in the popular mind.

There are very understandable reasons for the interest of American sociologists in Salem's year of travail, 1692. In contrast to Europe, all the American colonies had been remarkably free from serious trouble with witchcraft, although there had been a dozen or so sporadic cases in Connecticut and Massachusetts. Then, as the century was drawing near its close and just before the more rationalistic attitude of the eighteenth century was to prevail, this first major epidemic of panic occurred. Although the belief in black magic certainly lasted among the uneducated, the cases that reached legal trial after 1693 were indeed rare. The Salem calamity, consequently, has had the doubtful distinction of being a late example of a type of outbreak all too common in the centuries preceding it as well as of being the outstanding (and extremely obvious) example of the forces of superstition in the American colonies.

Far from blaming one man or one creed, modern theorists concerned with social behavior believe that such outbursts of witchcraft concurred with times of social and political unrest. Certainly Massachusetts at the time of the Salem tragedy was in a period of rapid social and political change as the economy turned from agriculture to maritime pursuits. During this same period, the Revolution of 1688 with its colonial repercussions, the loss by the New England colonies of their prized original charter, the struggle to secure a new one, and the controversy over the acceptance of the latter, were such momentous political changes that many colonists felt that their rights as English citizens had been lost. Even more apparent were various disasters that crowded one upon another during these perplexing years: the failure of Crops, some devastating fires, destructive Indian raids on settlements to the north, and severe losses at sea during the French War.

Not content with the hypothesis that economic, social, and political changes taking place in New England during the late seventeenth century made the colonists in their insecurity less stable in their judgment and more prone to emotional excitement, social historians have also sought more concrete explanations, both economic and psychological, to account for the acute troubles of 1692. One modern theory has tried to put the whole blame on greed: the accusers were trying to get the property of the accused. That such motivation may have entered into some cases cannot be categorically denied, but many of victims were the have-nots, the unfortunates of the communities involved. Indeed, when the accusations reached the wealthier and more capable members of society, many of them escaped, and the whole movement to find the guilty was quickly quashed. The other modern approach has been, of course, through our current knowledge of psychology. Here no single explanation suffices. Symptoms of mass hysteria, guilt complexes, and hypnosis can be detected in various cases. Despite occasional fairly obvious cases of simple imposture, evidence of what seems to have been monomania, hallucination, and mental telepathy appears frequently in the records of the trials.

When all the ascertainable facts concerning the Salem tragedy are put into focus, when all the explanations and theories are considered, some element of bewilderment remains. Seventeenth-century New Englanders appear to have slipped back mentally and socially as element after element in the cult of medieval sorcery turned up in the passion-ridden court of supposed justice. What seems to have started with mischievous children making trouble for a vulnerable servant rapidly became monstrous. At least once as many as thirty witnesses (and in many cases ten or more) testified against an accused witch.[4] Such accusations sometimes were made by innocent victims of what seemed to them sorcery, but frequently confessed witches deliberately implicated others or spoke against those already judged guilty. Insinuations of dark, unnamed evil accompanied confessions of dealings with the Devil (visible to his confederates as a little tawny or black man), of partaking in black ritual and witches' Sabbaths, and of being forced to sign the Devil's book. Tales of all sorts of torture inflicted on the "possessed" (and vouched for by many bystanders) included details of pin-sticking, pinching, scalding, and burning. More prosaic charges, often obviously afterthoughts concerning major or minor daily mishaps, of why someone's cow died or child had convulsions, are almost a comic relief, except that here too is apparent the lasting inheritance of medieval belief.

Hysterical excitement and terror undoubtedly seized many New Englanders in that tragic year of 1692, and this discomposure was not confined to the so-called ignorant or unschooled. Educated men also were confused at what could happen to a God-fearing people, and this wonderment lasted. As Cotton Mather somewhat pathetically commented a few years later, when the ferment had died down, "It was, and it will be, past all *Humane Skill* Exactly to *Understand* what *Inextricable Things* we have met withal."[5]

However bewildering the whole affair may have been, in one belief Cotton Mather never wavered: he was certain that the Massachusetts authorities were dealing, to the best of their ability, with witchcraft. He makes this certainty abundantly clear before, during, and after the main outbreak. Nor did he have any mental or emotional difficulty with the concept. The totality of faith that led to a visualization of his guardian angel time and again after his periods of prayer and fasting could easily extend itself to the acceptance of the claim that evil men and women could both see and enter into relations with that fallen angel, Satan. Privately, the young minister, who had just had the heady experience of being successfully in charge of the Old North Church for four years without his father's guidance or help, wondered if his accomplishment in leading many to God might not have made the Devil seek revenge; a few faithful parishioners also raised this question.[6] But more frequently, always a strong chiliast, he leaned toward the belief that the colony was going through the predictedly troubled period before the end of the world, a time when Revelation indicated there would be much witchcraft.

From his wide reading Cotton Mather knew very well that a few men, both in his own day and much earlier, did not believe in witches.[7] But such doubters, such fallers into the Sadducean heresy (of doubting the resurrection and the existence of spirits and angels), seemed to him undeniably questioning the truth of the Bible. Scripture told of witches and witchcraft; men were clearly instructed to put to death such sinners that entered into league with the Devil. Even if the word for witches had originally meant poisoners, a point of semantics discussed by scholars of the day, did not these modern, seventeenth-century witches try to poison man against God? Or these deniers of the existence of witches might be arguing that there had been witches in the old days. But no place in the Bible is there a time-halt on any sin.

In addition to the great question of heresy in any doubt of the existence of witches, in Mather's mind the doubters also showed a weakness in logic. Some people were obviously "possessed" in the sense that unseen forces were torturing them with physical and mental anguish. Why suppose that the Devil was acting directly when so many men and women were willing to confess themselves witches?

As a seventeenth-century Puritan, Mather could have rested his arguments on the Bible alone. But he did not. Accustomed as he was to consult theologically trained authorities to find their dicta on all perplexing questions, he reread—and occasionally copied into his books—the discussions on witchcraft in such revered scholars as Perkins, Bernard, Gaul, and Baxter.[8] Such men might disagree on lesser points and on methods of determining the guilty, but they all agreed that there were witches, as Calvin and Luther had so unequivocably held. When he turned to writers in his other field of lifelong interest, science, he found the same agreement, from Bacon to Boyle.

Nor did Cotton Mather in 1692 (or later) actually know anyone who did not believe in witches. Those antagonists who after the Salem events attacked him bitterly for allowing his credulity to inflame the witchcraft scare did not deny that there were witches. Both the mentally alert Thomas Brattle and the ignorant, confused Robert Calef carefully went on record as believing in the existence of witches; in fact, part of Calef's attack on Mather brought out that the latter had not properly urged the death penalty for confessed witches. Even when in 1711 the General Court of Massachusetts reversed the decisions of 1692 and compensated the victims (or their descendants), justice was done because of errors in accepting evidence against them at a time that the "Province was Infested with a horrible Witchcraft or possession of devels."[9]

Inasmuch as Cotton Mather was so very much in accord with his times in his acceptance of the ever-present danger of Satan's powers, his contemporaries certainly did not blame him for believing that New England could be plagued with witches. The question a few of them raised was whether he had not made the scare worse by his credulity in accepting too easily tales by women and children who were irresponsibly seeking attention. The implication also was there that he had done so for his self-aggrandizement in playing a part in these miserable dramas. Some years later criticism shifted to the question of whether he had made a sufficient effort to stop the cruel unfairness of the trials. Then, too, his steady claim from the beginnings of the trials that the judges were honorable men doing their best in a most painful situation did not make him popular with those who were emotionally involved with the unfortunate victims of the judges' mistaken zeal or even with those who just lacked his own great respect for authority.

Cotton Mather, with his good Puritan conscience, also questioned himself four years after the events as to his possible guilt in what he did or did not do when "the Inextricable Storm from the Invisible World assaulted the Countrey"; he was concerned especially about his "not appearing with *Vigor* enough to stop the proceedings of the Judges." He found he could clear himself; in fact, he felt that God had assured him that he was in no way blameworthy.[10]

Nevertheless, in more objective eyes that have the benefit of the perspective of later years, some of his lifelong weaknesses show themselves painfully in his dealing with individual cases of "possessed" children and women. His defensive wording in describing these cases indicates that some members of his congregation doubted the sincerity of the so-called victims; but Cotton Mather could not be deceived—or so he thought. Manifestly, he always had the ability to believe what he wanted to believe. As a result of this obstinacy, his questions to those claiming that they were being tortured by the Devil and his agents may have led to the answers he wanted. And in the case of unscrupulous and/or imaginative "victims," the possibility of imposing on him must have been obvious. The child that was so possessed by evil spirits that she could read a Catholic or Quaker book but not one by either of the Mathers or by John Cotton seems to be an amusingly obvious case of deceitful mischief helped by the attitude of the onlookers, among whom was Mather.

His credulity (which seems, of course, more ridiculous today than it did in the 1690s) was balanced most fortunately by his great sense of responsibility in keeping any taint of accusation from the possibly innocent. Here he could feel that he was admirably guiltless. The most outstanding example of this type of decent restraint on his part was connected with the death of his newborn son Joseph from a

birth defect. This sad event happened in March of 1693, still a time
of strain, with many reported as "possessed" by evil spirits. The
child's mother, backed by the gossip of neighbors, was certain that a
fright she had had from seeing a "horrible Spectre" on her porch
had caused the calamity; the grieving father thought that the malig-
nant deed, "this praeternatural Accident," was directed against him
for his success in leading his church. But he made no accusations,
accepting God's will.[11]

In his capacity as a minister, Mather followed the same policy of
restraint. The first person accused by the "possessed" Goodwin
children of torturing them was Goodwife Glover. She was sentenced
to die as a confessed witch, but first she told the minister of three or
four of her cronies who also practiced witchcraft (or believed they
did). After her death, the Goodwin children continued to be
"possessed" and told him of their new torturers. Each time he refused to divulge the names.[12] He wanted no false accusations, no
spreading of evil suspicion. (He realized, of course, that the
testimony of witches and even of the innocents "possessed" was
open to the gravest doubts; to accept as truth their statements came
dangerously near to believing in the veracity of Satan. Not all of his
contemporaries were so logical; if they had been, the Salem trials
would have come to a quick end.)

In other ways, too, Cotton Mather's actions were such that he
could later look back on them and not blame himself. As a
sinner—as all men are sinners—he believed that he had helped to
bring about the catastrophe of the withdrawal of God's pleasure in
the Elect and their resulting punishment; consequently he prayed
and fasted. But in a less general sense he honestly believed that he
had always been on the side of kindness and liberal fair-
mindedness.

He had been kind in individual cases, giving his time and efforts
unsparingly. His belief was that anyone seemingly suffering from
possession by the Devil should be separated from others so suffering, taken into a wholesome, religious home, and there by patience
and prayer helped back to normalcy. He tried this very rational
method in 1688 when the four Goodwin children were afflicted.
The eldest of them, a girl of thirteen, joined the Mather household,
for some time made everyone miserable by her actions, and then
overcame her demons to become an acceptable member of society.
When the Salem troubles began, he offered to open his home to six
sufferers, but his suggestion was ignored. In the cases of the two

young Boston women, Mercy Short and Margaret Rule, who claimed in 1693 that they were being tortured by witches and devils, he faithfully visited them, praying and fasting for their release; he also encouraged members of his congregation to keep long vigils, praying and singing Psalms to keep the evil demons from the sufferer's room. (The integrity of the two women has been much questioned, but this serious doubt of their moral standards at any period of their lives has nothing to do with Mather's efforts on their behalf.)

More important than these individual cases of charity was Cotton Mather's repeated plea that the greatest care be taken in determining the guilty. He followed his mentors, especially Perkins and Gaul, in rejecting many of the old folklore ways of deciding whether or not a person was in legion with Satan; for example, he spoke with scorn of the water test. He was less advanced in accepting the familiar notion that abnormal marks or extra "teats" on the suspect's body might be very indicative of too close a relationship with the Devil. The finding of puppets (little dolls made, perhaps, in the image of the victim-to-be) in the possession of the suspect also impressed him. But there remained other types of so-called proof that he felt called upon to explicate with some care.

The most disputed point of accusation consisted of what was called "spectral evidence."[13] The accused or the specter of the accused supposedly was seen doing evil deeds or taking part in gatherings of devils. Many thought that the devil could not use the shape of a good man in this way; therefore, the accused was guilty. The Massachusetts ministers, however, agreed that there was no proof of this limitation of Satan's power; in addition, the Bible provided instances of the possession of a good man by evil spirits. Accordingly, spectral evidence could be used to strengthen the case against a man or woman, but in itself should not convict. It was Cotton Mather who worded this advice for the benefit of the Salem judges; he also wrote privately to some of them to the same effect. (This caution was completely ignored in the hysteria of the trials.) It was his father, Increase Mather, who wrote in 1693 the most telling argument against relying on spectral evidence for conviction; his book, *Cases of Conscience*, helped to turn the tide of public opinion against the waves of accusation at Salem.

Less confusing than the spectral-evidence issue was the problem of confession. It was indeed satisfactory for the accused to confess to having signed the Devil's book, joined in midnight orgies, or done all sorts of evil to ungenerous or unkind neighbors or their children. But, as Cotton Mather noted carefully, under pressure and strain some unfortunates with disordered minds might very well imagine themselves guilty. Confession alone was not enough.

Then there was the problem of testimony by neighbors and erstwhile friends. Again caution was needed. Once a person was accused, many others sprang forward to accuse, remembering questionable acts and possibilities of the long past. Apparently no one had thought of witchcraft then. How much to be trusted was this sort of hindsight?

The best that Cotton Mather could offer by way of solution to the great difficulty confronting the judges (and all men of good intent) was that there should be all these types of evidence against the suspect before the verdict was given. If the person confessed, if other confessed witches implicated him, if two or more reliable witnesses had actually seen him do something or know something that showed supernatural power, if his answers in court showed much confusion, if there were suspicious marks on his body, if he owned puppets, and if, in addition, there was spectral evidence, then the judges might be confident that they were dealing with a witch. If he had sold himself completely to the forces of evil, then he should be put to death, for the safety of New England. If he was only slightly involved, then he should be punished, but he should escape the death penalty.[14]

This, then, was Cotton Mather's stand, and he never saw any reason to be ashamed of it: As the Bible, Christian scholarship, and observation of life showed, there were witches who harmed good people; less demonstrable, but obvious to him, these witches threatened to deliver New England back to the Devil, for it had been his property in pre-Puritan days, when the Indians held full sway. Kindness, prayer, and fasting were the best ways to treat victims who by no will of their own were in the power of Satan; and the efficacy of this method he had proved by the individual cases he had treated. It was possible, but extremely difficult, to determine who had actually entered into the Devil's employ, but good men owed it to other good people and to their country to try to perform this service. Every caution should be taken, especially in the moot question of spectral evidence. Looking back, he could see that the judges must have erred, but this failure was human weakness, not intentional evil. (And here he was being generous as they had disregarded his advice and suggestions.)

In judging the young Boston minister and his actions in the late 1680s and 1690s, many commentators leave the impression that this witchcraft episode, which took place while he was in his late twenties, was a dominant part of his life. Any consultation of his *Diary* and of a complete bibliography of his publications should dispel any such notion.

His journals for the five years before 1692 have been lost. But in 1692 his diary shows him much concerned with his ill health and excited about the return of his father and brother from England (after an absence of four years). He approves of his own courage in speaking out in a sermon against the prosecution of Quakers by the civil authorities. He notes "the horrible Enchantments, and Possessions, broke forth upon Salem Village." He tells briefly the story of his afflicted neighbor, without naming her—the Margaret Rule case that became the subject of his more detailed "Another Brand Pluckt out of the Burning." He composes a hymn and proudly includes it—with due humility, of course—in the diary. He resolves never to engage in personal quarrels, since they are a waste of God-given time.[15] And he saw his labors into print some nine times.

In 1693 events and shifting interests also came one upon another: he leads his church into the Half-Way Covenant, a step that called for considerable finesse. He plans and starts work on his three extensive scholarly undertakings, *The Angel of Bethesda*, the *Magnalia Christi Americana*, and the *Biblia Americana*. He is much concerned with two murder cases, mothers who had killed their bastards, and he tries to lead the unfortunate women to faith and repentance. A drought has to be met with prayer and fasting. A trip to occupy the Reading pulpit meets with the usual success. He helps Boston's Negroes organize a meeting. His son Joseph is born and dies, and the grieving father sees Satan's hand in the tragedy, a Satan angered by Cotton Mather's success in leading so many to God. Some pages of a sermon are mysteriously missing, notes lost on a trip to Salem that had the combined purpose of preaching and gathering material for a history of the "late *Witchcrafts* and *Possessions*" as part of his projected *Magnalia* (1702); again witchcraft is suspected. He is almost exposed to yellow fever, but a little miracle saves him. His two-year-old daughter, Mary, dies, but this time the grieving parent has a mystical experience that convinces him that all his children will be saved and await him in heaven.[16] And he manages to reach print only six times.

The diaries of 1692 and 1693 thus show Mather's customary con-

cern for the spiritual health of Massachusetts. Also clear are the in-
dications that he had caught the general fever and was inclined to
think in terms of witchcraft as the reason for various calamities. But
if Satanic "possession" and evil were issues of the day, they were far
from occupying all of his attention; he also had time for church
politics, scholarship, special sermons, and mystic experiences with
his Good Angel.

After 1693 the surviving diaries have remarkably few references
to witchcraft. He notes, of course, a day of fast held in January of
1697 throughout the province for New England's many sins: vanity
of apparel, sabbath-breaking, excessive drinking, etc.; and, in
Mather's words, "*Wicked Sorceries* have been practised in the
Land, and yett in the Troubles from the *Divels*, thereby brought in
among us, those Errors, on both Hands, were committed, which
wee have Cause to bewayl with much Abasement of Soul before the
Lord."[17] (Cotton Mather had drafted the original 1696 request of
the churches that a fast-day be held; this was approved by the
Massachusetts House of Representatives, but rejected by the Council because of an impolitic addition or "streamer" that the lower
house had attached to it. Samuel Sewall's bill to the same purpose
was then found acceptable.) But for the last thirty-odd years of his
life Salem is named in the diaries only as he mentions annual and
semiannual trips he made to this section of the colony. So, in October of 1696, he records:

> At *Salem*, on the Lord's-Day . . . I preached both parts of the Day, . . .
> with great Assistences. On Tuesday, I went as far as *Ipswich*, accompanyed
> with many Friends. . . . On Friday, I returned unto *Salem*, and on
> Satureday, unto *Boston*. A Journey full of Comfort, of Mercy, and of Ser-
> vice, and more than answering all my prayers concerning it.[18]

Other entries tell of his charitable gifts, usually books but occasionally money, that he sent to the poor of the struggling towns
north of Boston.

As the *Diary* suggests by its many hints of a very busy life,
Mather's publications on witchcraft compose a surprisingly small
portion of his total output. The fascination of witchcraft as an
aberration of the past has caused these items to be reprinted a
number of times, however. This fairly frequent reprinting is inclined to create two false impressions: the witchcraft books and
other connected items seem to be major, especially valuable
publications. As a matter of fact, they are hasty work, compiled in

the exigency of the moment, and so not nearly as interesting reading as many of his other books. Then, too, the reprinting of these items separately and in collections of witchcraft material makes them seem more numerous than they are. He actually meant for publication only two books that dealt mainly and directly with the problem.

The first of these, published in 1689 before the Salem outbreak convulsed the colonies, was *Memorable Providences, Relating to Witchcrafts and Possessions.* [19] This little volume is largely devoted to an account of the Goodwin children and their supposed affliction during the summer of 1688, of his taking the eldest girl into his home (and so separating her from her brothers and sisters), his close observation of her antics, and her return to normalcy as kindness and prayer repelled the evil forces in possession of her. If his gullibility in accepting the young girl's statements and acts as sincere is painfully (and sometimes amusingly) obvious, it is also worth noting that the book and his interpretation of what had happened had the endorsement of four other ministers of Charlestown and Boston; the 1691 edition, published in London, also proudly bore the recommendation of the great Richard Baxter. Of interest, too, are the comments of twentieth-century critics who see in Mather's treatment of the case much of the coming spirit of a scientific approach to all matters that had to do with the supernatural. His experimental method of practical tests as to the girl's reaction to various books, prayers, etc., his close observation of her actions, and, above all, his positive approach that she could be cured, all are more modern than medieval. [20]

In addition to the Goodwin case, *Memorable Providences* also contains six brief accounts of witchcraft which had occurred over the years in England and New England, a sermon occasioned by "what befel Goodwin's children," another occasioned by a suicide, and a fiery "vindication" of his father, who had been attacked by the Quaker George Keith. (In other words, Quaker attacks on Increase Mather were just as dangerous to New England's well-being as the Devil's other and perhaps more obvious attacks on the Elect through witchcraft.)

The second book of Mather's that dealt directly with the witchcraft outbreak was published late in 1692, at the end of the trials. *The Wonders of the Ivisible World*[21] was written at the request of Lieutenant-Governor Stoughton, with the idea that knowledge of the trials and of the mass of evidence against the con-

victed would justify the verdicts of the court. The essential part of
this short book recounts the trials of five of those accused, material
that Mather obtained from the clerk of the court. While *Wonders of
the Invisible World* has been much reviled as adding fuel to the fire
of suspicion going on, its late publication indicates that it could not
have been really influential in this way. Public opinion, aided and
formulated by Increase Mather's *Cases of Conscience*, which
appeared at the same time, had begun to swing against the acceptance of spectral evidence as proof of guilt, and the nightmare of
Salem was coming to an end; in fact, if Cotton Mather himself is to
be believed, his book met with a poor reception in the colonies (but
was read with interest in England).

Published with the *Wonders* were important excerpts from a brief
document or letter, dated June 15, 1692, usually referred to as "The
Return of Several Ministers." When it became unmistakable that
the Salem troubles were coming to a head, the governor asked the
ministers of the town churches for advice in dealing with this attack
by the Devil. The response to the governor's request, "The
Return," was signed by twelve clergymen but was actually written
by Cotton Mather, as he later stated. All apparently agreed that
suspects be treated with "tenderness" and with their privacy not
unnecessarily intruded upon; furthermore, no unlawful tests should
be given them. Spectral evidence alone should not be enough to
convict anyone, nor should the testimony of those who were
possessed by the Devil or had entered into contract with him be
accepted. Finally, with all these restrictions the judges should do
their best to determine and convict those guilty of witchcraft.

This notable semiofficial document, which was published in full
in Increase Mather's *Cases of Conscience* (1693), has been used to
show that Cotton Mather was not in accord with what happened at
the Salem trials. In such arguments the first part or the restriction
on the types of evidence to be accepted is stressed. But the letter
also has been used as grounds for the accusation that Cotton Mather
urged the judges to put to death all accused. In such arguments the
last part—really the last sentence—is stressed. Considered as a
whole, the letter shows its writer's firm belief that there were cases
of witchcraft in the colony, that every caution be used lest the innocent suffer, but that the judges should do their duty. The paper is
also of value as proof of Cotton Mather's statement that his stand
concerning the whole question was no different from that of the
other clergy.

In addition to the two books meant for publication, *Memorable Providences* and *Wonders of the Invisible World*, Cotton Mather wrote and allowed to be circulated in manuscript his accounts of two witchcraft cases that he had treated in 1692 and 1693. The first of these, *A Brand Pluck'd Out of the Burning*,[22] has to do with Mercy Short, a seventeen-year-old-girl who had been given a home as a servant after the loss of her own home. (Her parents and three of their numerous children had been slain in an Indian attack in 1690; Mercy and some of her brothers and sisters were then taken captive to Canada, but eventually brought back to New England.) Having affronted a witch one day in the summer of 1692, the young Mercy was afflicted with blindness and deafness (except to the instruments of Satan) and an almost complete inability to eat; she also was tortured by pin-sticking and burnings. Temporarily relieved, her sufferings took on new violence in November, and it was not until March of 1693 that the evil spirits were finally defeated. All this time she could have saved herself by signing (or merely touching) the Devil's book, but she remained steadfast while Mather and faithful members of his congregation prayed and fasted for her deliverance.

The second of these manuscript relations, *Another Brand Pluckt out of the Burning*,[23] tells the somewhat similar tale of Margaret Rule, another young woman. Her sufferings were borne in the fall of 1693. Again Cotton Mather—and many of his congregation—had no doubts about either the sincerity of the girl or the reality of her sufferings. But he apparently did not feel that any public benefit was to be derived from having the story reach the press. It was despite his express forbidding of such a step that Robert Calef printed in 1700 "Another Brand" as part of his attack on the Mathers, father and son.

The Mather-Calef controversy remains somewhat confused, with typical seventeenth-century name-calling on both sides. Mather always responded to adverse criticism with almost hysterical vehemence and with much grief that his usefulness to his fellow men would be impaired. He started to bring a suit against Calef, but changed his mind—God helped him "to forgive and forgett the Injuries done" to him.[24] On the other hand, Calef wrote so incoherently that *More Wonders of the Invisible World* (1700) leaves a stronger impression of its author's own peculiar and confused mind than of the sins of the ministers of the Old North Church. Calef seemed to be accusing the Mathers of encouraging rather than quieting the witchcraft scare; he added various innuendos about Cotton's morals.

In trying to evaluate Calef's arraignment of Mather two points have to be kept in mind. First, the anti-Mather faction, for it is often supposed that Calef had support against the Mathers, preferred to remain unnamed. On the other hand, Cotton Mather had the open backing of the grateful father of the Goodwin children and of prominent members of his congregation, for Calef's *More Wonders* was answered by them in *Some Few Remarks upon a Scandalous Book, against the Government and Ministry of New England written by one Robert Calef . . .* (1701). Secondly, the whole attack (and counterattack) came well after the actual scare, for Calef's confused book was not gathered together until 1697 and not published until 1700 (and then in London, for its backers may well have realized that colonial presses would be unwilling to be responsible for its printing). The terrors of 1692 and 1693, looked at with hindsight a few years later, seemed very different from what they had been during the tense emotion of the epidemic of supposed cases. And by this late date the errors of the witchcraft judgments were fully acknowledged; Calef was writing for a cause already won.

Calef's attacks induced Cotton Mather to write to him a number of times. One letter, with the attestations of six witnesses as to what had happened in the Margaret Rule case, was printed in *More Wonders;* another was summarized in the same book. Mather also supplied a lengthy letter to *Some Few Remarks.* These later defenses are only indirectly part of Mather's contribution to the literature of the 1692 outbreak.

Cotton Mather's planned publications on witchcraft remain two: *Memorable Providences* (1689) and *The Wonders of the Invisible World* (which bears a 1693 date, but was actually in the public's hands by the end of 1692). To these may be added "The Return of Several Ministers" (1692), which may be regarded either as the joint thinking of some twelve ministers but written by Cotton Mather or as written by the latter and agreed to by the other ministers. To these regularly printed accounts of cases and statements of Mather's beliefs may also be added the two manuscript accounts that Mather allowed to be circulated:*A Brand Pluck'd Out of the Burning,* which did not reach print until the twentieth century; and *Another Brand Pluckt,* printed by Calef's unfriendly means in 1700. There are also extant at least four letters in which Mather discussed or touched upon the subject; two of these are to the judges serving at the trials. The letters, of course, were not meant for publication, and they serve only to reiterate his stand: there were witches, spectral evidence was not to be depended upon, great caution had to be exercised lest the innocent suffer, but the judges had to do their duty.

Mather's later accounts of the witchcraft outbreak are what he considered to be necessary recapitulations of the same material. When in 1697 he wrote the life of his late friend and parishioner, Sir William Phips, the governor who had at first sanctioned the trials and later ordered the courts to stop the prosecutions of the accused witches, this chapter in Phips's short reign in Massachusetts could not be omitted, and in Mather's loyal eyes the governor had to be defended. Nor could he ignore the subject in his 1724 biography of his father, for it had been Increase Mather's *Cases of Conscience* that had acted as a powerful determinant in shifting public opinion against the acceptance of spectral evidence, a development that had really brought the trials to an end. These biographies cover the Salem outbreak briefly; Cotton Mather's history of the colonies in the seventeenth century, his *Magnalia Christi Americana* (1702), quite fittingly has a longer account or rather accounts. A section devoted to individual cases of witchcraft includes the story of the Goodwin children. Although he had planned and started his own account of the Salem troubles, he used instead a work by a close, sensitive observer of the trials, the Reverend John Hale (1636 - 1700). The latter made available to him a manuscript of a book on the subject, *A Modest Inquiry*, which was ready for the press in the late 1690s but which was finally published posthumously in 1702.

In these three works, the two biographies (of Phips and Increase Mather) and the *Magnalia*, are to be found Mather's only substantial retrospective views of New England's witchcraft tragedies—and one of these was not by his hand even though it appeared as part of his record of the history of the colonies. After 1693 and the fairly rapid quieting of the Salem furor, Cotton Mather apparently was not at all preoccupied by the subject. Even when Calef's scurrilous book appeared in 1700 and loyal members of the North Church answered it, their pastor's emotion, put on the ground of possible impairment of his usefulness, was about the attack on his father and himself.

On the other hand, the Salem tragedy by its very nature and extent was not one that permitted itself to be completely forgotten or ignored. From time to time Mather would express his bewilderment and sorrow about "the errors of our Dark Times." He was not without sympathy for the victims of the miscarriages of Salem justice and for their descendants; for example, when in 1709 a number of the accused that had survived and the families of some of those put to death appealed to the government for justice and amends, he preached before the General Assembly, effectively urging their cause. And for many years he could not free his mind completely from the question forced upon sincerely religious New Englanders: the "meaning of the Descent from the Invisible World" that suddenly came upon them in 1692; almost twenty years later he was still asking the Lord for an answer. He had, however, learned one lesson. From the beginning of the witchcraft outbreak in Massachusetts he had been wary that under emotional stress false charges of trafficking with the Devil would be made against the innocent; now he felt the need of a definite warning that no one, especially in illness, should make haphazard accusations against the more unfortunate members of the community. For example, in *The Angel of Bethesda*, a volume of medical advice he was composing in the early 1720s, sufferers from nightmare (which Mather believed came from indigestion and flatulence) are plainly told:

And it has been too Common a Thing, for People under the Invasion of this Malady, to imagine a *Witchcraft* in the Case; And anon perhaps the Folly proceeds unto the Accusation of a poor, mean, ill-loved old Woman in the Neighborhood. *Away, Away*, with such Idle Fancies. (153)

Cotton Mather rather enjoyed feeling that he was abused by his contemporaries. Nevertheless, however often he complained that his daily good deeds, his constant efforts to reform people by his writing—his best efforts to serve God and man—went unappreciated, he could not suspect that his "enemies" in the nineteenth century would link his name firmly with the stigma of Salem witchcraft, holding him responsible for what he did not do to restrain his contemporaries from putting the suspected witches to death as well as for what he did write that may have aggravated the general tension and terror of 1692. Nor could he imagine that the semiliterate of the twentieth century, one step further from the truth, would hazily think of him as the cause and villain in the Salem tragedies. Confident that during the witchcraft cases in both

Boston and Salem he had followed the dictates of reason, faith, and love of one's fellow man, he faced posterity with his seventeenth-century conscience clear.

CHAPTER 7

Magnalia Christi Americana

O F all Cotton Mather's many publications, his *Magnalia Christi Americana*[1] is the one that later generations of students of American secular and church history have praised and attacked even as they have used it. No study of the northern English colonies can ignore this storehouse of information, for there is little of seventeenth-century New England that is missing from the two ponderous volumes. The plans that made possible the great migration from old England, the settlement of the various colonies, the political and religious leaders, the all-important founding of Harvard to provide future generations of leaders, the tenets of New Englnd Congregationalism and its church organization, with duly discussed schisms, the ways God had revealed Himself by individual providences, the menacing Indian wars—the whole story as seen by a clergyman of the 1690s is there. Along with patent political and religious history, much of the changing social and cultural life of the period is observable, always by implication and sometimes by worded detail.

The modern reader, however critical of the historical sense, credulity, and self-proclaimed impartiality of the compiler of all this material, is at least convinced of the latter's sincerity: Cotton Mather believed that he was writing the truth; in Christian charity, not quite the whole truth because he began with the idea that it was his duty to skim over the tales of some of New England's troubles and trouble-makers, not even naming the men, and occasionally women, involved; nor did he feel called upon to dwell upon the sins of ministers who fell from grace. But this virtuous if not very scholarly restraint soon gave way to his anger as he thought of the Quakers and Seekers who had perturbed the struggling saints and their congregations. For example, he does not see Roger Williams as a democratic visionary whose teaching would be an inspiration to America. To Mather, "a whole country in America was like to be set on *fire* by the *rapid motion* of a windmill, in the head of one particular man . . . a preacher that had less *light* than *fire* in him . . ." (Vol. II, 495).

If such scathing judgments now seem evidence of wrongheadedness, they are, together with equally surprising eulogies of long-forgotten ministers and scholars, indicative of the book's peculiar strength. Mather did not see issues or the services of individuals as later writers on New England have viewed them. He does give the varying viewpoints of the seventeenth century: his own proud account of those he did not doubt were the good men, the heroes of the occasion, as they struggled to found the churches and to keep the colonies alive; and by his acrimonious attacks and by the very points he feels he has to stress as well as the acts he had to vindicate, he implies with some clarity the opinions of dissident factions.

It was in 1693 that Cotton Mather conceived his project[2] of helping his own and future generations by preserving in print recollections of the first settlement and early development of New England. By May of 1695 he was able to publish, as a sort of advance sample of the work to come, *Johannes in Eremo,* the biographies of five of New England's especially distinguished preachers. With these lives was an "Advertisement," a four-page "schaeme" of the forthcoming *Magnalia.* By this time, then, he had the whole work adequately planned. As can be judged by the *Johannes in Eremo* publication, he saw no advantage in having material appear for the first time in print in the *Magnalia.* On the contrary, he finally included seventeen of his other publications. Of these only five had been written before he started the *Magnalia;* the other twelve, appearing separately in print between 1695 and 1700, seemingly were planned to serve a double—really a triple—purpose, often having been pulpit offerings (and printed as such) before their inclusion in this major work. He also drew upon his other publications for occasional paragraphs or brief illustrations. Very occasionally, too, he used material from other hands without editing or rewriting.

The manuscript must have been fairly complete by the end of 1696, for the Reverend John Higginson of Salem, called upon as one of the oldest surviving ministers in the colonies, dated his prefatory attestation to the book's worth and truthfulness March 25, 1697. Mather then added the "General Introduction" in the summer of 1697. According to the author's calculation his labors had taken only two years, but he seems to have tended to minimize the time in order to stress his own expediency: he wanted all to know that he had accomplished speedily this extensive work even as he preached three or four sermons a week, carried on his usual pastoral duties, published lesser books, and gathered material for his two other comprehensive projects, the *Biblia Americana* and the *Angel of Bethesda.*

Despite the eagerness of the author to have his completed work before the public, at this point there were necessary delays. Before he was able to send the *Magnalia* by safe and sympathetic hands to London for publication, he had the completed manuscript with him for three more years, a wait that incidentally gave him ample time for revisions and corrections. Then there was a further postponement while his friends in England struggled to have the lengthy manuscript printed.

Finally, after many prayers and days of fasting for the safety of his work, Mather was rewarded. Copies of the *Magnalia* reached Boston in October of 1702.[3] The seven books that comprised the folio were paged separately, but the whole formed a volume of nearly eight hundred pages, printed, except for the first fourteen pages, in double columns.

1   Book I: "Antiquities": The Founding of New England

The first book shows that Mather had some knowledge of earlier exploration and attempted settlements on the Atlantic coast, but his real interest, quite properly, considering the avowed purpose of his work, lay in the New England colonies—Plymouth, Massachusetts Bay, Connecticut, and New Haven. In telling their not-uncomplicated stories, he manages with considerable skill to give the multiplicity of settlement that took place during the first twenty-five years of colonization. He was well aware of the many clergymen who, having been silenced in England for their dissenting practices, came to New England, often accompanied by loyal families from their former congregations. These groups did not simply go from an English town to construct an American town; there was much shifting around and resettlement as economic needs and difficulties in adjustment to fellow settlers became apparent. The early history of New England is the story of many towns that were developed almost simultaneously, and this phase of the settlement Mather handles with clarity as he depicts the rapid growth of the colonies.

As a Bostonian, Mather was also inclined to stress the importance of New England's largest city, the capital of Massachusetts Bay Colony, and, in his words, "*THE METROPOLIS OF THE WHOLE ENGLISH AMERICA*" (Vol. I, 91). Consequently he felt called upon to append to the chronicles of the settlement of the various colonies a so-called history of Boston. Although it mentions briefly such calamities (and signs of God's anger) as epidemics and fires, this previously printed account, a lecture-sermon[4] delivered in 1698, devotes much of its emphasis to a plea for the latter-day inhabitants to turn back to God and His true church.

II Book II: The Lives of the Governors

Like most men of his era, Cotton Mather saw history in terms of outstanding leaders. Consequently, Book II of the *Magnalia* traces the development of the four New England colonies)later three when Connecticut and New Haven became one) in terms of their governors. As he covered the century to 1686, substantial biographies of the first, well-known governors are followed by shorter sketches of their often less known successors. For Plymouth, he writes at length of William Bradford and only briefly of the three men that followed him, Edward Winslow, Thomas Prince,[5] and Josiah Winslow. Even in the short accounts, however, he carefully notes the main services to the colony of each man. For example, Mather, always interested in forwarding education, points out what seems to him to have been Prince's outstanding achievement: his procuring money for the establishment of schools. By way of explanation Mather notes that this governor knew the value of an education, for his "*natural parts* exceeded his *acquired*; but the want and worth of acquired parts was so sensible unto him, that Plymouth never had a greater Mecaenas of learning in it" (Vol. I, 115).

After merely naming the magistrates that served in Plymouth, Mather goes on to the great governor of Massachusetts Bay, John Winthrop. Again he gives brief accounts of the lesser men who followed Winthrop: Dudley, Haines, Hopkins, Vane, Endecott, Bellingham, Leverett. Then, varying his pattern, he lingers with the life of Simon Bradstreet. Again he merely names the magistrates. The pattern is the same for Connecticut, with Edward Hopkins, his abilities and bodily infirmities, discussed at some length. For New Haven, Theophilus Eaton is the great man to whom the account is devoted. When New Haven and Connecticut were joined, the dominant figure is the second John Winthrop.

At the end of this section, too, Mather destroys the balance of the book by appending another former publication, a lengthy life of the late governor of Massachusetts Bay Colony, Sir William Phips. The author's excuse is that he is offering such an example of "heroic virtue" that it would have been "little short of a vice" to omit it.

III   Book III: The Lives of the Divines

The third book of the *Magnalia* must have been a true labor of love, if ever there was one; Mather's efforts, moreover, were not in vain, for this part, the lives of the English-born, first generation of colonial ministers, is the most readable section of the whole work. Granted that Mather of course was familiar with his admired Plutarch's general precepts in writing biographies—the value of comparisons and parallelisms, the use of distinguishing characteristics to make each subject stand out clearly, the stress to be put upon the ethical significance of each life—the task facing this "American Plutarch" (as he has been somewhat mockingly called) was indeed difficult. Mather had to tell life after life of good men whose careers necessarily had many similarities, but each of whom upon close consideration had particular strengths and abilities. Rather than remain silenced in England and so unable to serve God and His people, a good many Puritan ministers and candidates for the ministry emigrated to America, most of them to New England. According to Mather's calculation, some seventy - seven of these men, practically all graduates of Cambridge and Oxford, had held pastorates in the mother country; another fourteen came over before the completion of their preparation for the ministry; still another fourteen, again English university men, came over after the Restoration; some twenty more Mather was forced to classify as "anomalies," a few of whom were Anabaptists and Episcopalians, and some of whom fell by the wayside, proving "disserviceable" to the churches (Vol I, 235 - 38).

It is interesting that even by the end of their own century many of these men, the outstanding leaders in their little churches and communities, had become mere names in the history of individual churches. Of the 125 or more divines who came to New England in her first fifty years of settlement, Cotton Mather was able to gather information about only fifty-odd, with his data far from evenly full.

Consequently, he made no attempt to keep his biographies of an even length. When he knew much, he tells much; when he knew little, he gives what scant outlines he can.

When his facts permit, Mather follows a more or less set pattern in his accounts. For each man he identifies family background, always commenting upon remarkable rises from poverty or admirable connections with the nobility. The proper education of a minister was a very important subject for Mather (as well as a status symbol), and so he takes care to include as much as possible about each man's training, with emphasis, of course, on his college or colleges. As a fellow minister (writing an ecclesiastical history that would be read by church-minded people), the biographer carefully lists churches in which each pastor served and what parts of the Bible he covered or stressed in each pulpit. Whenever possible, his actual preaching is appraised, with comments on such points as extensive preparation, frequency of text-citing, typical length of sermon, and the use of rejection of notes as a pulpit aid. If there were any publications, these are faithfully noted, whether or not Mather had actually seen the books or sermons. Children and wives usually seemed of less interest, although wives that were the daughters of ministers and sons who became ministers were duly remarked upon.

But whatever else Mather had found out about his subjects, a decided fondness for the details of last illnesses and for death-bed scenes is all too apparent. Frequently these painful ends are fairly moving as final evidence of a Puritan saint's utter faith or at least of his preoccupation with the tenets of his church. The much-admired Reverend Richard Mather, for example, spent his last hours in a death-bed discussion of the Half-Way Convenant (Vol. I, 455 - 56). Of all Cotton Mather's good men, only poor George Philips, the Watertown minister, met a somewhat undignified end: "He laboured under many bodily infirmities: but was especially liable unto the *cholick;* the extremity of one fit whereof, was the *wind* which carried him afore it unto the *haven* of eternal rest, on July 1, in the year 1644 . . ." (Vol. I, 379).

As might be judged from the strained wit of the respected Philips's passage to a better world, Cotton Mather did his best to make his biographies enjoyable. Whenever the name of a minister allowed him to play upon it, he indulged his typically seventeenth-century wit. The Reverend Ralph Partridge afforded the perfect opportunity. Duxbury's church had an eagle in Partridge, who in England had been in the state of a hunted partridge, and throughout his life he had the innocency of a dove, until he took flight to become a bird of paradise (Vol. I, 404 - 405). Although the continued transformation of Partridge is an extreme example of Mather's laborious skill, other names also lent themselves to metaphorizing. The Reverend Henry Flint proved to be a solid stone in the foundations of New England until he became a glorious one in the walls of the New Jerusalem (Vol. I, 443). The Reverend Samuel Stone, on the other hand, distinguished himself by being in his principles both "A *Load-Stone* and a *Flint-Stone*" (Vol. I, 435). The unfortunate Reverend Samuel Whiting, noted for his accuracy in Hebrew and his elegance in Latin, had suffered as the victim of "ecclesiastical sharks" that "drove this Whiting over the Atlantic sea unto the American strand." Nevertheless, so full of faith was this good man that he "would have thought himself a fish out of his element, if he had ever been at any time anywhere but in the Pacifick Sea" (Vol. I, 504, 508).

But Cotton Mather was not content with using his wit in this way to individualize his subjects. Somewhere in each biography he cites a particular characteristic or a typical incident that gives the man life. Fairly often the attribute has to do with the subject's ministry. The Reverend Jonathan Burr preached as if he were already in heaven (Vol. I, 373). The Reverend Samuel Newman, more concretely, was "a very lively preacher and a very preaching liver" (Vol. I, 430). The fortunate Reverend John Fisk possessed in his first wife a "godly and worthy consort" to serve as his concordance, her expertness rendering any other biblical concordance in his library useless (Vol. I, 478). The Reverend Thomas Cobbett's strength lay in his effective prayer:

That *golden chain*, one end whereof is tied unto the *tongue of man*, the other end unto the *ear of God* . . . our Cobbett was always pulling at, and he often pulled unto such marvellous purpose, that the neighbours were almost ready to sing of him, as Claudian did upon the prosperous prayers of Theodosius—*O Nimium Dilecte Deo* [O thou, too much beloved of God] (Vol. I, 520).

Sometimes, too, the outstanding point is some special ability or combination of abilities that goes beyond the pulpit or prayer-closet. Mather quotes at length the Reverend Nicholas Noyes's account of the Reverend James Noyes and the Reverend Thomas Parker, in which much is made of the excellency of their singing and their extraordinary delight in singing psalms, a practice they indulged in publicly four times a day on the Sabbath and privately every day after evening prayers with their families (Vol. I, 485). Perhaps less gifted but much more versatile was Thomas Thacher, minister and physician at Weymouth and Boston, whose skill in Hebrew enabled him to compose a lexicon in that language; he could also write in Syriac and "other oriental" characters; nor was his skill limited to these old languages, for he was "a most incomparable *scribe*" who "wrote all the sorts of hands in the best copybooks then extant, with a singular exactness and acuteness." Added to these abilities was a "certain *mechanic genius*, which disposed him in recreations unto a thousand *curiosities*, especially the ingenuity of *clock-work*, wherein at his leisure he did things to admiration" (Vol. I, 490).

Not all of Cotton Mather's praise is so specific. The comment can be more general praise of scholarship and ethical strength, as in his brief and unconsciously amusing tribute to the Reverend Daniel Denton:

Though he were a *little man,* yet he had a great *soul;* his well-accomplished mind, in his *lesser body,* was *an Iliad in a nut-shell.* (Vol. I, 399)

The Reverend John Allin also affords a pleasing picture:

He was none of those low-built thatched cottages, that are apt to catch *fire:* but, like a high-built castle or palace, free from the combustions of *passion.* (Vol I, 461 - 62)

The lives may be decorated in this way with many a metaphor to bring out the worth of these first occupants of New England's pulpits, but whether Mather knew much or little about his subjects, he kept close to the men's lives and careers. His asides are amazingly few. True, John Sherman's twenty-six children tempt him into considering other large families (Vol. I, 517). A discussion of John Eliot's service to the Indians brings in a fairly short reflection on childbirth among the savages (Vol. I, 559). Similarly, in a later discussion of a Harvard graduate, the Reverend Urian Oakes, the very name starts a brief oak tree - druid digression that culminates in a picture of Harvard College as "a rendezvous of Happy Druids" (Vol. II, 16). But these interpolations are the exceptions. The life and accomplishments of one man follow another's with remarkably few interruptions, until the author has exhausted his information.

IV   Book IV: Harvard College: Laws, Benefactors, Eminent Graduates

As the first preachers passed away, New England's churches would have been hard put to have their pulpits filled if Harvard College, established for that very purpose, had not supplied new generations of young men aspiring to the ministry. Therefore Mather devoted the fourth book of the *Magnalia* to the college, a catalogue of its graduates. The actual founding of the college, its benefactors, and its early vicissitudes are briefly treated; on the other hand, a few of President Increase Mather's Latin commencement addresses on the value of colleges and the meaning of degrees are loyally cited at some length. The requirements for the bachelor's and master's degrees are also included, in Latin, just as the young candidate would have read them. Then follow very full accounts of the lives of nine ministers, all Harvard men. The tenth life is another of Cotton Mather's appendixes of somewhat variant material. This one is a reprinting of his life[6] of his younger brother Nathaniel, Harvard 1685, a model of early piety and scholarship, who had died at the age of nineteen.

After the tribute to Nathaniel at the end of Book IV, a decided break in the pattern and continuity of the *Magnalia* appears. The first four books are devoted mainly to Puritan leaders. Not only is there psychological interest in the way of thinking and the careers of these men, but their common dedication to Congregationalism and to the survival of the New England colonies gives these first books a type of continuity. The last three books, however valuable in historical content, do not hold the imagination of the modern reader in the same way.

V   Book V: Church Polity and Organization

The fifth book contains the "Faith and the Order in the Churches of New-England" as agreed upon in synods held sporadically after 1642. Here Mather may be said to be more editor than author as he gives the conclusions concerning points of belief and of church organization upon which the majority of New England's ministers at different times found themselves able to concur. Following the more general topics are explicit questions and answers, again based on synodal discussions and decisions. The questions are indeed varied and practical—and no different from the ones that churches have debated in other ages. Is it lawful under any circumstances for a man to marry his wife's sister? (Never.) When is divorce justified? (In cases of natural incapacity, the discovery of a living previous partner, uncleanness, incest, malicious desertion.) When may a minister give up his work? (Only because of incapacity.) When may a minister break the bonds of the private confessional by telling a man's sin? (For the safety and protection of others.) May usury be practiced? (Yes, regulated by the laws of charity.) (Vol. II, 252 - 69).

VI Book VI: "Illustrious, Wonderful Providences"

The sixth book is of a completely different nature. Here Mather, showing credulity to a degree that has earned him the scorn of later eyes, has gathered together the "wonders" or "divine providences" that had punished or rewarded the people of New England. It is worth noting, however, that this undertaking, an attempt to prove that Providence, not chance, is all powerful, had been urged by the ministry from time to time during the preceding forty years, notably in 1658 by Matthew Poole, the noted biblical scholar, and in the early 1680s by Increase Mather. Again in 1694 the Fellows of Harvard College had petitioned for cooperation from the clergy in supplying material for such a worthy project (Vol. II, 341 - 42). Consequently, some of his fellow ministers supplied Cotton Mather with tales of remarkable occurrences that seemed to them to prove God's direct methods of punishing and rewarding His children. That a compilation of these stories of supernatural interference in daily life was thought necessary by the clergy seems to indicate an age of rising doubt. On the other hand, Cotton Mather was not alone in his willingness to see God's hand very concretely in what others might call accident.

The first type of remarkable event covered, sea deliverances, must have struck close to the heart of many living in these maritime colonies. The last tale of this type, gentler than some, is a very pleasing one: A "praying and pious company" on a sloop ran out of food on a journey from Fayal, one of the Azores.

God sent his dolphins to attend'em; and of these they caught still one every day, which was enough to serve'em [seven men]; only on Saturdays they still catch'd a couple, and on the Lord's Days they could catch none at all (Vol. II, 354).

Finally, with a "holy *blush*" that pious (but not exactly quick-witted) company ceased fishing on the Sabbaths.

From deliverances at sea, Mather goes on to other remarkable rescues, then to the effect of thunder, outstanding conversions, and noteworthy judgments on sinners, fit fates descending upon those guilty of drunkenness, Sabbath-breaking, disobedience to parental desires, contentiousness, lust, dishonesty, prayerlessness, etc. Much of this denunciation becomes the usual preaching against the sins of a decadent New England; in fact, Mather is using three of his sermons,[7] one on thunder as the voice of God, two on the necessity for man to fear God. He adds to this previously printed material still another of his publications, a history of criminals executed in New England between 1646 and 1698.[8] These doleful tales have the professed purpose of serving as warnings against sin and against living in circumstances that may lead to grievous sin; in some cases the emphasis seems rather on the remorse and turning to God of doomed sinners that had come under the influence of a good minister, by obvious implication Cotton Mather.

Abruptly the whole question of sin and the result of evil-doing is left as Mather turns to a completely different type of remarkable occurrence: the spread of the Gospel among the Indians. Here again he is serving as editor rather than author, for he includes an account that he had been given of the Christianizing of the Indians on Martha's Vineyard; then the progress of missionary work in other parts of New England is very sketchily covered. This apparently happy subject of Christian influence upon the natives was not without its warnings to any of the latter who hesitated to accept the teachings of the church. Any "obstinant infidel" was certain to lose his family and home by painful means, even if he chanced to survive long enough to see the errors of his ways.

From Indians, good and recalcitrant, Mather goes to "wonders of the invisible world." Here he gives twelve cases of apparent witchcraft or possession by an evil spirit: women having fits; families being attacked by stones, bricks, and sticks, thrown by invisible hands; apparitions appearing after death; and the account of the afflicted Goodwin children previously given in his *Memorable Providences* (1691). After thus proving that devils and their in-

struments are strong and numerous the author cites a single case of
a good angel, one that evidently supported Mrs. John Baily in her
last hours on earth. As the fourteenth wonder, Mather returns to
New England's evil spirits, but the following brief history of the
Salem troubles of 1693 is not by his hand. Recognizing that he had
a controversial subject to deal with, he had every reason to believe
that his source was a reliable one and above question. The authority
to whom Mather openly turned for the account was the Reverend
John Hale, who as minister of the neighboring town of Beverly had
been in close touch with Salem events. The manuscript which Hale
made available for the *Magnalia* was also published separately in
1702 under its author's name.[9]

For the casual reader this sixth book is undoubtedly the most confused part of the *Magnalia*. But for the author and compiler of this
varied material there was a clear, unifying lesson running
throughout it: the quick and obvious reward of the good and the
even more rapid, more striking punishment of nonbelievers. Obviously an afterthought, the following appendix has remarkably little to do with the rest of the book. These five favorite stories of
precocious, very religious children who died young in great faith
had appeared in Mather's *Token for the Children of New England*
(Boston, 1700), and some of them had been included also in earlier
publications. Five months or so after having the manuscript of the
Magnalia taken to England, Mather sent this addition to be inserted.[10]

VII   Book VII: "The Wars of the Lord": New England's Tribulations

In Mather's eyes, the seventh book, like the sixth, had a strong
central theme, in this case the manifold dangers that the colonial
churches had undergone. He always believed that New England's
sins were responsible for her troubles, including the attacks made
upon her border settlements by the native savages. Therefore he
begins with dissensions within the churches. Factions had tried to
lead the faithful astray. Difficulties had ranged from the underpay-
ment of ministers, to points of church organization, even to
threatened heresy. Misled congregations had almost slipped into
too-rigid separatism, the theory that each church was a complete
unit. (The conservative point of view—and Mather's—was that the

churches were independent in structure but should seek and accept
the advice of their brother churches when difficulties arose; Mather
was a particularly strong advocate of synods.) And there had loomed
the double threat of misled men turning toward familism,
overemphasis upon grace (and doing away with the ordinances of
the church) or turning toward antinomianism, a stressing of the
value of good works for man's salvation (rather than predestined
election). The Quakers, too, had tried to change Congregationalist
doctrine. Still another peril lay in the possible contamination of the
church by impostors, uneducated and sinful men who posed as
ministers. Mather was the more vehement in exposing this not very
common or acute hazard because he himself had been temporarily
deceived by one such pretender to the pulpit.

Finally Mather reaches the penalty for New England's sins: the
Indian wars that had long endangered and were still threatening the
very existence of many of the settlements. The final section of the
book treats, fairly briefly, events through King Philip's War, stopping in 1676. For an appendix to this last book, the author for once
makes a basically apt choice when he uses his *Decennium Luctuosum*, originally published in 1699, a detailed history of the Indian wars from 1688 to 1698. In both the original printing and the
Magnalia, the history itself is followed by a sermon. Unfortunately
for the apparent organization of the *Magnalia's* seventh book, the
Decennium Luctuosum devotes only twenty-eight of its thirty sections to the struggle of the colonists against the native savages. The
twenty-ninth section is an attack on Quakerism, a threat to
Congregationalism that Mather had dealt with earlier in the book
he was now compiling.

Mather felt that the dangers to New England's true churches
were far from over, and on this favorite theme the *Magnalia* ends.
The thirtieth chapter of the *Decennium Luctuosum* is devoted to a
prophecy of New England's downfall if reform did not come and
come quickly. The sermon that follows repeats this bitter lesson: the
colonists are to expect the worst of fates unless there can be an end
to "idleness, drunkenness, uncleanness, cheating, lying, prophane
swearing, and, above all, that which is the *root* of all, the profana-
tion of the Lord's-day" (Vol. II, 681). Then there is a typically
Mather last-word warning. Do not accuse others. Let every man
look to his own life, his own family. On this note of dominant gloom
but possible hope of reform Mather's great book ends.

VIII   *Critical Reaction to Mather's American Epic*

As the undertaker of this attempt at recording New England's first century of settlement and development fully realized would happen, his work—despite its high level of purpose—has met with a mixed reception. Cotton Mather dedicated this, his first important book, to the service of Christ. In the opening lines he paraphrased the beginning of the *Aeneid,* deliberately suggesting that here is another great epic of a heroic struggle. For years he prayed and fasted for the printing of his work so that he would know his efforts were not being rejected by God. Nevertheless, not only in their own day were the thick folio volumes both admired and mocked, but later critics also have held very varying opinions, having praised while they admitted serious faults, have attacked while they acknowledged that the book has too much value to be ignored.

To comment on the book's obvious lack of unity is, of course, to comment upon Cotton Mather's fundamental outlook upon society as well as upon his method of work. He saw each colony and indeed each church as a separate foundation; these essentially separate u- nits originally were bound together only by a most worthy, dedicated first generation of settlers and by such good common enterprises as the establishing of Harvard. From his contemporary viewpoint, each church and each town retained its identity, even though all were threatened by such common dangers as Indians, Quakers, witchcraft, and worst of all, a general religious decline. He also saw all history in terms of good leaders and evil corruptors. Working hastily in his spare hours on copious material that was too near to him for perspective, he struggled to get as much as possible of the New England story preserved both for its examples of true faith and virtue and for its warnings of the penalties of sin.

The *Magnalia* plainly lacks objectivity, that modern *desideratum* of historical and biographical studies. Cotton Mather was too devotedly a descendant of the Cottons and the Mathers not to gloss over any weaknesses in his ancestors and even in the admired colleagues of his forefathers; their opponents in church and political matters had to be wrong. Even at this early stage in his develop- ment in tolerance, he could admit that there were good men of all Protestant persuasions and that these men should be one in fellowship before God. Nevertheless, he was too closely associated (by descent and service) with the Congregational Church to look

with generous eyes on what he regarded as threats to its very existence: the activities of the Quakers and, toward the end of the
century, the establishment of the Church of England in Boston. He
was too loyal a New Englander not to resent any encroachment on
the liberties of the colonists by the royal governors. He was too
much of his own time, hearing daily tales of the barbarous sayings
and kidnappings committed by the savages, to see nonconverted Indians as other than devils-incarnate. Fortunately for later generations of readers, Mather was far from being a subtle man; all his
biases are evident, almost blatant, and so can be taken into consideration in any attempt to formulate from the *Magnalia* a true picture of the colonies in their early years.

It is no impugnment of the basic honesty of Mather's work to
note that there are numerous minor errors of fact; for example, occasionally the natal town for one of the English-born ministers has
become distorted and his lists of early magistrates for the different
colonies have lapses. The possibility for slips was ever present, as
Mather was well aware. Information given by friends and relatives
often may have been inaccurate, as such recollections understandably are. Given what he considered a reliable source, usually a
fellow minister, Mather seemingly accepted without question any
tale he was told. But by no means can all errata be attributed to his
informers. Mather was no research student carefully checking his
facts; on the contrary, he was inclined to rely upon his memory or
his father's recollections of the past. These failings undoubtedly account for some weak spots, although there may have been genuine
difficulty in getting accurate data about such very different confused affairs as early controversies within particular churches and
the shifting reports and suspicions about the Indian wars.

The *Magnalia* as we know it suffered in one more way: neither
the author nor his English friends who arranged its publication were
given any opportunity to proofread. How far the printed text differs
in detail from Mather's manuscript remains a question, but the
author endeavored to correct some slips by inserting a list of corrections into such copies as the American bookseller had on hand after
the first sale.

Although he neglected to take time to check his facts with the
true historian's proper diligence, Mather did take great pains to
make each point clear and effective. In his introduction, as was his
unfortunate habit in his books that he expected to be read by his
fellow ministers (and especially by interested scholars in old

England and Scotland), he overdisplayed his learning with one reference or quotation piled upon another. For example, he covers the whole field of classical history from Herodotus to Plutarch in less than two pages. Once he has proved his scholarship, he is content in the body of the book with strengthening his points aptly by fairly frequent but not really excessive quotations from many sources. Historians, church fathers, and theologians are regularly called upon for aphorisms and illustrations, but lines from Virgil, Horace, and Seneca also brighten many pages; less often, but occasionally, English poets contribute wisdom and example, "Old Chaucer," Milton, Butler, Dryden, and the much-admired Blackmore being quoted. Not only was Mather strengthening his points but he was also offering, according to his avowed purpose, nuggets of knowledge for his reader to mull over.

His other obvious way of making his points outstanding was by his choice of wording. His most common rhetorical device relies on some form of repetition, often accentuated by alliteration.[11] Again and again, Mather uses two or three words or phrases where the modern writer would limit himself to one. Sometimes there is repetition of meaning, sometimes duplication or echoing of sound, sometimes added qualification. Prophecies are fulfilled "precisely and exactly"; the hand of Heaven is "evident and undoubted," while the dispensations of the Creator are "various and marvelous"; in the fear of God there is "reverence, respect, and regard"; a satisfactory sermon is "holy and humble"; a learned minister has a "competently good stroke at Latin poetry"; Indians become "threatening and raging"; worldly men have "advancements and advantages"; the faultless John Cotton possessed a "clear, neat, audible voice, and easily heard in the most capacious auditory."

Usually Mather's plays on sound and meaning are meant in all seriousness as simple emphasis. Once in a while, however, he deliberately puns in order to evoke a smile at man's shortsightedness. So he comments that parsimonious congregations liked their ministers to be stars rather than mere lamps, "provided, like the *stars*, they would *shine* without the supply of any earthly contributions unto them" (Vol. II, 491.) Or he remarks that some of the "chief worthies" of the colonies were content to defend their beliefs with "easie pens," with the only effect "a little harmless and learned *ink-shed*" (Vol. II, 500).

This habitual verbal ingenuity for emphasis, plus the steady use of citation and quotation for illustration, has caused modern critics to discuss at some length Mather's baroque style, at its height in this particular book. His method of trying to reach his readers certainly is striking (and distressing to many ears), especially in our age of plain writing. It should be noted that the types of elaboration that Mather used were popular in the Elizabethan period, and survived to a degree in the work of some seventeenth- and eighteenth-century authors. What made the style of the *Magnalia* remarkable in its own era and almost astounding in later years is the remarkable frequency of the same literary devices.

With all its admitted weaknesses and foibles, the *Magnalia* has received remarkably high praise (often even as it was being censured) by critics who have looked upon it from very different points of view.

Moses Coit Tyler, famous for his pioneering study of early American literature, becomes amusingly guilty of some of the faults he found in the *Magnalia* as he vehemently attacks Mather for his "tumultuous, swelling, and flabby declamation," his "infinite credulity," and his inability to be objective (the last a failure that caused him to stain "the chaste pages of history"). Having somewhat recovered his equanimity, Tyler goes on to admit that this book, "the most famous book . . . produced by any American during the colonial time" has great merits as well as "fatal defects," for in its "mighty chaos" is much that helps the reader to paint for himself a living picture of the great days of New England.[12]

Barrett Wendell, a Harvard scholar of the old school and a writer known for his felicitous style, admits the independency of the parts of the *Magnalia*, its incredible superstitions and hasty errors; among its stylistic weaknesses he lists prolixity, the frequent use of pedantic quotation, and the occasional employment of fantastic conceits. Nevertheless, after reading in it for eleven years, he rates the book "among the great works of English literature in the Seventeenth Century." Two hundred years after the book appeared, Wendell found every line lucid and no paragraph tiresome; he particularly enjoyed the individuality of separate portraits of New England's ecclesiastical and political leaders. In the opinion of this later historian of New England's thought, Cotton Mather has succeeded—and this was his great accomplishment—by his outstanding "veracity of spirit" in making his reader feel the Puritan ideal.[13]

Kenneth Murdock, another noted social historian, biographer, and critic whose main interest has been New England, also comments on the formlessness of the whole book, calling it an "historical collection" rather than a history; he, too, recognizes its errors of fact, slips in names and dates, even occasional misinterpretations of characters and events (perhaps due in many instances to Mather's proximity to the events under discussion). But Murdock praises the "skill in biography," the "good narrative" that is so frequent, and the unity of individual books.[14]

Sacran Bercovitch, an outstanding, imaginative scholar and critic of early American literature, refuses to cavil about the *Magnalia's* possible flaws and really rejects any consideration of the book as history. To him it is an "essential part of American letters," an artistic creation, an American epic that foreshadows Whitman's *Leaves of Grass*, with "a style that provides a fitting Cloth of Gold" for the great theme.[15]

On the other hand, it was as social history that the *Magnalia* was selected in 1963 by leading scholars to be in the White House Library, some eighteen hundred books selected from the vast output of three hundred and fifty years of American writing as a "working library for the presidents of the United States."[16] In fact, Cotton Mather's history or epic, as you will, is the only representative in the library of the thinking and writing of colonial New England.

CHAPTER 8

Bonifacius (Essays to Do Good)

B *ONIFACIUS. An Essay Upon the Good, that is to be Devised and Designed, By Those Who Desire to Answer the Great End of Life, and to Do Good While they Live* (1710),[1] commonly referred to as *Essays to do Good,* is a direct reflection of Cotton Mather's deliberately planned and dedicated life. Consequently, the book is closely related to his *Diary,* with its persistent and ever-burgeoning emphasis on good deeds and, especially in certain passages, to his unpublished autobiography, *Paterna,* which is based on the *Diary.*

In contrast, however, with the *Diary,* which records one type of good deed only to jump to another type, from the small act of charity to the extensive beneficent plan, the *Essays to do Good* is an organized attempt at social reform. The earnest author tries to show how all classes of men in their various occupations (and even in their leisure) can serve God and man. Occasionally, as was his way, Mather allowed his thoughts to stray from his planned structure, but as a whole the essay is clear and the development of its points logical.

This comprehensive attempt to help others to be good necessarily was far broader in its scope than the sermons that he from time to time had devoted to what seemed to him especially urgent reforms. Some of these sermons, nevertheless, he made obvious use of in appealing again for New Englanders to change their ways. And in no chapter in his little book does Mather forget to remind his reader that every Christian is a temple of God; therefore service to man is service to God, a guiding rule that his parishioners heard repeatedly from the Old North pulpit.

The extended project to organize the ways everyone can serve God by benefiting his fellow men may well have been given its impetus at this time by the rising fervor of Mather's enthusiasm for the German pietist movement with its stress upon practical goodness.

On the other hand, he had the example of at least two fairly recent English books of somewhat similar purpose. Almost certainly Mather was familiar with Richard Baxter's *How to do Good unto Many, or The Publick Good is the Christian's Life*, first printed in 1682 and then as part of a 1707 posthumous collection of Baxter's works in which Cotton was reading in 1709. (Baxter was an old family friend and mentor, often respectfully cited by both Increase and Cotton Mather.) Despite its title, this earlier manual is a general consideration of man's duty, lacking the concrete suggestions with which the *Essays to do Good* fairly teems. Very probably Mather also had read *Essays upon Projects* (1697) by Daniel Defoe, the noted pamphleteer with whom he proudly corresponded. This lively, readable book offers remarkably modern solutions to a good many problems of civilization, including fair taxation, useful highways, care of the weak-minded and insane, the education of women, and the protection of sailors aboard ships; but despite its brilliance in spots, Defoe's brief volume is lacking in unity and orderliness; then, too, its emphasis is on the desirability of the reform rather than on the method of accomplishment. Of the three "do good" books, Mather's is the most effective in its organization of helpful suggestions for every moral, thoughtful man to act upon daily and so bring about needed reforms.

Before getting to the main subject of the *Essays to do Good*, Mather is carefully explicit about the Calvinist doctrine that man is saved by grace, not by good works. (This basic tenet he had reiterated, of course, many times both in his sermons and in his other publications.) But having been saved by grace, a good Christian demonstrates his faith by his deeds. In Mather's judgment so essential is this result of faith that "the motto on the Gates of the Holy City is: 'None But the Lovers of Good Works to Enter Here' " (p.30). Apparently no one is to experience in the hereafter the joys of the New Jerusalem or the Holy City of God[2] who does not properly evaluate (and presumably therefore perform) good works. "Yea, to be *saved* without *good works*, were to be *saved* without *salvation*" and "*Heaven* is begun upon *earth* in the doing of them" (p. 30).

Mather also felt that any attempt to better the world should start with self-examination of one's own "heart and Life." Consequently, he reminds his reader to consider at night (and especially on the "Lord's-Day evening") his actions of the day, to question whether he has he has used properly his blessings and benefited from his afflictions. Has he employed to the best advantage any hours of forced leisure by reading good books or perhaps by planning good deeds?

Having pondered upon his own weaknesses and presumably corrected them, the "useful man" will now "enlarge the sphere of his consideration" to his relatives. With one of his happier puns Mather announces, "One great way to prove ourselves *really good,* is to be *relatively good"* (p. 41). "Relatives" start with the immediate family. The foremost duty of a husband and of a wife is to see that each is saved and growing in character. Mather naturally is able to be more specific about the man's obligation: the minister of the Old North Church is speaking for himself as he asks, "What shall I do that in my carriage towards my wife, the kindness of the blessed Jesus towards His Church, may be followed and resembled?" (p. 42). But the good husband will ask his wife to help with the answer.

The parents then must be "continually devising, and even travailing, for the good" of their children—that they may be wise, educated, lovely, polite, and serviceable, and with "generous, and gracious, and heavenly *principles"* in order to be able to resist temptation. For the method by which children can be encouraged to reach this admirable state, Mather is frankly autobiographical as he quotes at length (pp. 45 - 52) from his *Paterna* his own theories of child-raising, theories that are also to be found in his *Diary.* The fond father explains again how his children were prayed for, told "delightful" biblical stories at meals, catechized, and taught to pray and to get along with each other and with outsiders.

As a careful and loving father of children of various ages, the busy head of the family had many other duties: supervising their reading and writing, punishing them (by refusing to teach them something or not allowing them in his presence), helping them in their troubles, and having them taught a practical avocation as well as trained academically. (He believed that both boys and girls should be given enough "insight into a skill" to enable them, under necessity, to earn a livelihood by it; although he offered as possibilities the limners' or the scriveners' or the apothecaries' trades,[3] he was certain that each child's own inclination must be the determining factor in making a choice.) From time to time the children were summoned individually to him and asked to consider their spiritual state if death should claim them immediately. Finally, as the children matured, he added to (or planned to add to) his efforts on their behalf every endeavor "for their best accommodation in the married state," with his prayers and labors for "the *espousal* of their souls unto their only Saviour" taking precedence over his care for their temporal circumstances.

Included in Mather's concept of the family are slaves and servants. The question of slavery and especially the refusal of so-called Christians to assume the proper responsibility for the souls of their slaves had disturbed him for some years. He had preached and written upon this subject previously, most effectively in a 1706 published sermon, *The Negro Christianized.* He now drew upon this material to make an impassioned plea that masters and mistresses lead to Christ those for whom they were responsible. To strengthen his appeal, he uses a double argument, part threat, part promise: if these "poor *slaves* and *blacks*" should be of the Elect of God, think, then, of the sin involved if they are lost through a master's negligence. On the other hand, whether of the Elect or not, when Christianized the slaves would be better servants, more faithful, industrious, and submissive (p. 53).

Mather reiterates two more points that he had made earlier about the morality of slavery. He begs again for an act from the British Parliament ordering all colonial plantation owners to see that their slaves were instructed in Christianity. And he concludes with a protest that the slave trade is a "spectacle that shocks humanity" (p. 54).[4]

His plea for kindness to servants is also taken from an earlier publication, this time from one of 1696, *A Good Master Well Served.* A good master should assume a fatherly attitude toward his servants. In other words, he ought to teach them as much as they can absorb and he should do his best to lead them to Christ. The lack of gratitude in people always seemed to Mather a very common sin, and so he reminds masters and mistresses that they should be grateful for the services done for them and take care not to forget these former services when the servant is old and so has "small failings" (pp. 54 - 55).

Relatives who are not part of the immediate family do not hold Mather's attention long, but he has much to say about helping neighbors, both spiritually and practically. Being generous with the poor and the ill is not enough; true charity must take another course. The good neighbor tries to find employment for the idle: "Find 'em *work*; set 'em to *work*; keep 'em to *work. Then*, as much of your other bounty to them, as you please" (p. 60). The good neighbor also sees that poor children receive some education—at least taught to read and to know their catechism. All this (and much more) is to be done without thought of gain or gratitude, in fact despite recrimination and abuse.

As a way of encouraging "Good Neighborhood," Mather proposes a method that he had used to strengthen his own church: the organization of societies, "tried and strong engines to uphold the power of godliness" (pp. 63 - 64). His first suggestion, a simple enough one, is that a dozen or so "associated families" hold meetings to pray, hear sermons repeated or newly preached for their benefit, and sing Psalms. As these families would be bound in "one bundle of Love" they would be "serviceable unto one another" in times of affliction or temptation. And varied opportunities to do good would occur to them (pp. 63 - 65).

For a second type of society, "Young Men Associated," Mather had developed fairly set rules of conduct from his own experience with such groups, and these he now offers to the general public. The two-hour meetings of the young men should include, of course, two prayers, a "repeated" sermon, and perhaps a Psalm. Carefully acting under the minister's guidance, the members were to be "charitably watchful" in their attitude toward each other. Unrepentant sinners were to be expelled, and absentees who did not respond to "loving and faithful admonitions" were to be "obliterated" (from the club's register). Every three months there should be a collection; every two months a meeting should be devoted to the problem of the rising generation and the future of the church. During their discussions every taint of "backbiting and vanity" should be avoided; hence points of practical piety should supersede any discussion of affairs of government and other "disputable and controversial matters." As a last—and very practical—point of duty, each young man should seek other young members-to-be so that the parent society could "*swarm* into *more*" (p. 68).

Near the end of the *Essays to do Good* Mather returns to this favorite subject of his with a third way that men can combine in doing good, "Reforming Societies or Societies for the Suppression of Disorders." Such organizations of mature men, presumably of some standing in the community, were active in England and to some extent in the colonies. Cotton Mather can again offer his own happy experience with their effectiveness. As their very name implies, these societies had as their first concern the elimination of vice, fraud, and oppression. The Boston interpretation of their purpose obviously went beyond any attack on evil to the doing of good deeds of a more positive nature that could include the relief of an afflicted neighbor, the distribution of good books, and even the erection of charity schools.

Having discussed what good every man, no matter what his position in the community, can accomplish, Mather then devotes his ingenuity to the particular ways men of different professions and occupations can develop their own virtue and what types of good deeds they can accomplish. (He breaks this pattern only once to consider the ways in which churches may do good: after self-examination to see if they have fallen into evil, they should consider working for a stock or treasury that could be used for the propagation of religion, perhaps by the dispersing of good books among the poor or by aiding new congregations.)

Many of Mather's suggestions as to how men of different professions can be good and do good are obvious: ministers are urged to benefit by their own preaching, to be faithful in their pastoral visiting and catechizing; magistrates should enact good laws and back the ministry; doctors should take care of the poor as well as those able to pay; rich men should be generous, giving at least a tenth of their incomes to charity. Surprisingly often, however, along with all these to be expected platitudes there is a vivid turn of phrase or image that should make any reader think (or smile). So ministers are told that they might become better church leaders by asking themselves, "If an angel were in flesh, as I am, and in such a post as I am, what methods may I justly imagine, he would use to glorify God?" (p. 69) And by thinking of themselves as the wind that "feeds nobody, yet it may turn the *mill*, which will grind the *corn*, that may feed the *poor*," conscientious clergymen may remind themselves to keep a list of the poor always with them when talking to the rich (p. 78). Rich men, in turn, should not hoard all their money for their sons, since the latter may not be willing even to buy tombstones for their parents.

Sometimes, too, Mather makes a telling point that shows considerable acumen and kindly wisdom. For example, when asking schoolmasters to be gentle with their students, he notes:

It is boasted now and then of a *schoolmaster*, that such and such a *brave man* had his education under him. There is nothing said, how many that might have been *brave men*, have been destroyed by him; how many *brave wits*, have been dispirited, confounded, murdered, by his *barbarous* way of managing them (p. 87).

Again, physicians are asked to remember that many sick people can be cured by the expectation of being freed from burdens, by the consolation of religion, and, in general by "bright thoughts." The suggestion this time is gently made: "*Tranquility of mind* will do strange things, towards the relief of *bodily maladies*" (p. 103).

As it proposes the good courses that men of different professions should be following, the reforms they might bring about, the ethical principles that must govern their acts, the *Essays to do Good* necessarily reflects many of the evils that were shocking men in 1710. Thus magistrates and rulers are begged not to misuse their God-given power; more specifically, they are not to act for their own gain—the ideal Christian governor certainly did not take bribes. Lawyers should be scholars and wise men, keeping constantly a "court of chancery" in their breasts lest they do anything that their consciences forbid. Thus aided, they will "abhor to appear in a dirty cause" (p. 127), but they will appear for "oppressed widows and orphans"—and if they have become wealthy by any "*dishonest* and *criminal* ways," then "excessive fees must be disgorged by Restitution" (p. 129).

Most of the *Essays to do Good* seems to be directed toward concrete problems of its author's immediate world of Boston and Massachusetts, but Mather is not content to conclude his book without extending it to a more general "Catalogue of Desirables." Many of these are indeed broad in scope: the propagation of the true Protestant religion; an endeavor to eradicate the "lamentable" ignorance and wickedness to be found in Wales, in parts of Scotland, in Ireland, in the Near East; the moral improvement of sailors, soldiers, and tradesmen; the founding of universities in which true piety will prevail; and the multiplying of charity schools. The important issues of the day, Mather felt, then resolved themselves to be the reviving of primitive Christianity, the persuading of European countries "to shake off the chains of popery," and a "Quickening" of the spirit of good people (p. 142).

In contrast to these somewhat nebulous and grandiose goals appended at the book's end, the body of Mather's little manual is a very down-to-earth consideration of what people of good will can do to improve the society they live in. Undoubtedly this homely, practical tone has helped to make the *Essays to do Good* the most popular of all Cotton Mather's many books. One indication that the book was read and, although it had appeared anonymously, the author recognized may be seen in Benjamin Franklin's fourteen

Dogood papers,[5] the first of which was published in the *New England Courant* of April 2, 1722. The young author of these essays, much influenced by Addison and the *Spectator* papers, was making his own ironic commentary on various phases of life about Boston and Harvard, but he created as his mouthpiece Mrs. Silence Dogood, who described herself as "an Enemy to Vice, and a Friend to Vertue . . . of an extensive Charity, and a great forgiver of *private* Injuries." Did he not expect his readers to think of the *Essays to do Good*, to smile at the thought of its author who was not regarded as quick to forgive personal injuries to him (or his father) and was never known to be silent about any topic?

Another sign that the book found an audience and had enough life to be in some demand a hundred years after its first appearance may be seen in its frequent reprintings in inexpensive editions during the first half of the nineteenth century.[6] At least eighteen editions, bearing only the title *Essays to do Good*, were published between 1807 and 1845, sponsored not only by Boston, New York, Philadelphia, London, and Glasgow printing houses but also appearing under the aegis of firms in such smaller cities as Johnstown (New York), Wilmington (Delaware), Lexington (Kentucky), and Portsmouth (New Hampshire). Although most of these editions were in modernizations of Cotton Mather's language and with some omission of points thought to be outdated, his main ideas remained of interest.

In some contrast to the reception of the *Magnalia Christi Americana*, which from its first appearance had its admirers and detractors, Mather's *Bonifacius* or *Essays to do Good* has enjoyed a surprisingly steady chorus of praise. The keynote of this tribute to the book's effectiveness may be seen in Benjamin Franklin's repeated acknowledgment[7] that his career of usefulness had found much of its initial inspiration in Mather's little book. As a very young man, Franklin found himself the possessor of a worn copy of the *Essays to do Good;* looking back in later years, he realized that no book had done more to give him the overall principle of watching each day for the good that could be done and then questioning himself at night whether or not he had accomplished his end.

More specifically, Franklin in forming his well-known junto seems to have used Mather's idea that young men should organize themselves into societies. Organizations of this nature could serve many purposes, but not the least of these would be the development and clarification of the member's ideas. (This proposal of course was not original with Mather; such clubs had existed earlier and were generally popular in the eighteenth century.) Like Mather, Franklin was quick to admit the danger that discussion groups might fall into pointless bickering and arguing. Both men felt that this pitfall could be avoided if men took care and were not too positive in their speech. Unlike the older Boston minister, the young politician and statesman-to-be naturally felt that political questions as well as moral and philosophical ones should come under consideration.

Men of later generations often have regarded the systematic and businesslike goodness of both Mather and Franklin as vaguely offensive in the little leeway that was allowed for spontaneity of spirit. (This complaint could be applied with equal truth to much of the thinking of the eighteenth century, the age of reason and practicality.) Nevertheless, despite Mather's deliberately organized approach to virtue, critics have had much to say in favor of his *Essays to do Good*. Moses Coit Tyler,[8] writing in the 1870s, forgets his usual annoyance with Mather to speak of the little manual's "clear ingenuity"; in fact, he claims, it is "a book which holds the germs and hints of nearly all those vast organizations of benevolence that have been the glory of the years since it was written." Barrett Wendell,[9] passing judgment twenty years later, is most impressed by Mather's devotion to "combined, co-operative effort" as the means of improving society.

Recent critics have been appreciative of Mather's felicitous style in this little book of practical instruction; Thomas J. Holmes,[10] for example, finds it to be "warm, friendly, helpful, encouraging." Nor has the Mather-Franklin connection been ignored. Arthur Bernon Tourtellot[11] in a recent essay has considered at some length the formative influence of the older man on the younger in the latter's general approach to life: the concept of using all hours not devoted to one's trade or profession to reading; the recognition of the beneficial value of societies or voluntary associations that would foster "mutual responsibility and mutual inspiration" for one another's welfare; the importance of steadily doing good not only for mankind in general but also for one's own happiness.

Unfortunately for his own contentment, Cotton Mather was always convinced that he went through life with is fervent devotion to devising ways to help mankind completely unappreciated. The repeated praise during the eighteenth century and down to our own age of his *Bonifacius* or *Essays to do Good* for both its purposeful content and its readability is therefore pleasantly ironic, since no book could be a more direct reflection of its author's constant efforts to serve his Creator and to help others to serve Him through serving their fellow men.

CHAPTER 9

The Christian Philosopher

C OTTON Mather finished compiling *The Christian Philosopher: A Collection of the Best Discoveries in Nature, with Religious Improvements* in 1715; as he often did with his more valued publications, he sent the manuscript to London for publication. His English friends did not succeed in having the book printed until 1720, when it appeared bearing a 1721 date.[1] Like Mather's other important publications of his later years, *Bonifacius* (1710) and *Manuductio ad Ministerium* (1726), *The Christian Philosopher* is surprisingly compact, some 304 pages in all.

The little volume is heavily and obviously dependent upon the leading scientific thinkers of the day. Consequently, it reveals both the accuracy (and inaccuracy) of factual knowledge in natural science at this time and the theories then being promulgated as scholars and would-be scholars gathered new facts through more accurate observation and experimentation. It also briefly presents the scientific theories formerly held and now being rejected by more advanced thinkers. In other words, the book is a summation of what a generally well-informed man living in the first decades of the eighteenth century would know about his universe, from the sun overhead to the worms crawling underfoot.

Considered from the more personal viewpoint of Cotton Mather's development as a believer and thinker, *The Christian Philosopher* is proof that estimates of the Boston clergyman based on his early publications and even on his great opus, *Magnalia Christi Americana* (1702), are grossly unfair. He may always have looked back regretfully at the religious fervor and dedication of his grandfathers and their contemporaries, the first generation of New Englanders; certainly he never renounced his Calvinist creed. Nevertheless, he changed with the times, perhaps more than he fully sensed.

The purpose of *The Christian Philosopher* is stated and restated,

in the introduction and in every chapter or essay, as the author called his divisions. The reader is to learn that the wonders of natural
science (in Mather's eighteenth-century terminology "natural
philosophy") prove to reasoning men that their world had a most
superior Creator. In this general theme that man's growing
knowledge of science supported religion rather than weakened it,
Cotton Mather was very much in accord with most of his fellow
members of the Royal Society—at least with their published
statements. (Hints of any unorthodox private reservations held by
some members on such difficult questions as the Trinity presumably
had not crossed the Atlantic, and so Mather's overwhelming respect
for all members of the society was undisturbed.)

If he was thus happily in agreement with Newton, Boyle, and the
other distinguished members of the Royal Society, he also unwit-
tingly came very close to the philosophic approach of the very
group of anti-Calvinists that he scorned, the Deists. Although he
always thought of himself as supporting the tenets of his church
against deistic attacks on Calvinist orthodoxy, in his stress on the
Creator as the efficient cause of everything in nature, on the
supreme design of the universe, on the general and particular
benignity of God in all his creations from planets to insects,
Mather's thinking cannot be distinguished from early Deism.[2] (Only as the deistic movement developed was there a weakening of the
emphasis on God's continuing part in the creation of man's world.)

The Christian Philosopher makes no defense of Calvinism; the
plan of the book did not call for any theological argument *per se.*
On the other hand, by implication, Mather's God of 1715 no longer
is an arbitrary Ruler, choosing His Elect, keeping careful account of
the sins of the faithful and the damned, using natural phenomena to
threaten, to teach, to punish. In earlier volumes, a man who broke
the Sabbath would have his children drown the following week;
every time one of his own children became ill, Mather's diary
reveals that the fond father wondered what his sin had been. A
people's sins were punished by a calamity of a larger scale, an
earthquake or flood; and New England had to reform her worldly
ways back to her earlier concentration on religion if she hoped to
avoid catastrophe. The later Cotton Mather may still occasionally
wonder whether natural catastrophes are not God's threats or
punishments; on the other hand, he is often content to see natural
forces as symbolic—the thunder turning man's thoughts to God's
power. In the general impression that *The Christian Philosopher*

makes upon the reader, the Calvinist concept of an arbitrary God of personal retribution has largely given way to a creative Power, an all-wise God Who has provided a wondrous universe for man; and only through reason can man know this God.

The plan of the book is relatively simple. After an introduction, there are thirty-two essays or chapters, in the traditional organization of natural philosophy then thought to be Aristotelian. Mather begins with astronomical topics: light, stars, the sun, various planets (Saturn, Jupiter, Mars, Venus, Mercury), and comets; "Of Heat," not very logically, is an appendix to "Of Comets." With the moon briefly waylaying him on the way, he then comes down to earth. He is largely discussing physics and meteorology as he considers rain, rainbows, snow, hail, thunder and lightning, air, wind, and cold; then he adds some geology and mineralogy for his discussion of the "Terraqueous Globe" with its gravity, water, earth, magnetism, and minerals. His last chapters are botanical, zoological, and biological, rising step by step from vegetation through insects (which include frogs and toads), reptiles, fishes, the "Feather'd Kind," and quadrupeds to the climactic "*Lord of this lower World*" (p. 221), for whom all has been created. And to man he devotes his longest chapter, over eighty pages.

Each chapter or essay attempts to cite or quote the leading authorities in the field. Occasionally and briefly he acknowledges older writers and theories, but his interest is in the new science. He fully recognizes Newton as the outstanding thinker of the period, whose theory on any scientific or philosophic question should be noted most respectfully. In Mather's effusive words, the "illustrious" and "incomparable" Newton is the "Perpetual Dictator of the Learned World," from whom " 'tis a difficult thing to dissent in any thing that belongs to *Philosophy*" (p. 41).

Newton is cited frequently, but Mather also depended on the works of other contemporary scholars; again and again he cites or quotes from John Ray's *Wisdom of God Manifested in the Works of the Creation* (1691), William Derham's *Physico-Theology* (1713), George Cheyne's *Philosophical Principles of Natural Religion* (1705), and Nehemiah Grew's *Cosmologia Sacra* (1701). He still has high praise, however, for the encyclopedic labors of one earlier writer, Heinrich Alsted (1588 - 1638), whose books were old favorites with the Mathers. All these writers in turn cited and quoted from many quthors, English, French, and Italian. This material Mather used, usually without indicating that he was not completely familiar with the original work. This practice made his work seem even more learned than it actually was, an impression that Mather would not scorn. Nevertheless, it should be remembered that he did not doubt the accuracy or interpretation of the "industrious" Mr. Ray, the "inquisitive" Mr. Derham, the "ingenious" Dr. Cheyne, and the "illustrious" Dr. Grew, all of whom he looked upon as respected colleagues in making scientific discoveries.

To the information that he thus amassed from others, he from time to time inserted, especially in the "terraqueous" essays, additional material that he had gathered and sent to the Royal Society. The most important of these observations concerns cross-pollination of different types of corn and of gourds and melons (pp. 124 - 25).

In each essay Mather uses his material and cites his authorities to show the remarkable characteristics and the perfect adaptability to purpose of a part of Creation. Sometimes he interrupts the lesson to cry out in praise of the Creator. For example, in "Of the Stars," after noting that through the telescope man has learned much about the universe, he exclaims:

> *My GOD, I cannot look upon our Glasses* [telescopes] *without uttering thy Praises: By them I see thy Goodness to the Children of Men!* (p. 17)

Less typically, in "of Magneticism" he offers a "digression," quoted at length from Robert Boyle, the noted physicist and founder of the Royal Society: if man is puzzled by the principle of magneticism but can see it in operation, why should he not accept the union of "gross Body" and "immaterial Spirit" in man, a doctrine beyond our understanding unless man makes his "Reason Pupil to an *omniscient Instructor*," or, in other words, accepts Revelation (p. 111).

Having quoted and paraphrased his authorities, at the end of each essay Mather always returns to his overall point: every part of creation proves the existence of a superb Creator. The conclusion may be a paean of praise, such as "*O infinitely Great GOD, I am astonished! I am astonished!*" (p. 166) or "*Great GOD, on the Behalf of all thy Creatures, I acknowledge in Thee we move and have our Being!*" (p. 88). Sometimes the earnest author can develop a fairly elaborate and not very surprising metaphor; for example, the ending of the essay on magnetism, in which souls of men are iron (cleansed, not rusty, and at first passive) and the Savior is the lodestone (pp. 115 - 16).

The astronomical chapters are brief and give the impression that

Mather struggled to give all the information he could find or could make comprehensible to the average reader. When he reaches the more observable parts of nature, he seems to be selecting from his sources. In "Of Minerals" he rejects any discussion of fossils since they are but the "Exuviae of Animals," then asserts that there are "near twenty sorts of earth," but takes time to mention only potter's earth, fuller's earth, and chalk. There are "a dozen several sorts of stones" found in large masses—of these, he comments briefly on slate, marble, freestone, limestone, "warming stone," grindstone, millstone, and whetstone before going on to stones "found in lesser masses" and jewels, to salts, bitumens, "mettalick Minerals" ("about a dozen," but only mercury interests him), and metals; here he does little with iron, almost ignores silver, and devotes himself to gold, its peculair qualities as a metal and its benefits and dangers to man. In the zoological chapters the same plethora of information is apparent, with the author arbitrarily choosing what he will develop.

In his thirty-second and last essay (pp. 221 - 304), Mather reaches the climactic part of his dissertation, reaching new heights both in factual material included and in religious fervor. Although he moves rapidly from point to point, he obviously wants to include every fact, detail, and theory that will advance his thesis. He is using, obviously, his lifelong interest in medical lore and his eager reading in the more modern science of anatomy to validate his basic assertion: reason teaches that the "workmanship" (a favorite word with Mather) of man's remarkable body proves the existence of a most superior Creator. Only at the end of the essay (and of the book), as he dwells upon this God and especially upon his Son, the Savior, does the attempt at a reasoned approach give way to emotional ecstasy, but even then he brings himself back to a final struggle to corroborate by reason the great Christian doctrine of the Trinity.

Man is to be considered both as the Temple of God and as "a *Machine* of a most astonishing Workmanship and Contrivance" (p. 222). He starts accordingly with man's body as being "most obvious." First of all, man's upright posture is praised, and this stance is made possible partially by his feet, so "exquisitely accommodated" in construction that they "*trample Atheism under foot*" (p. 223). Before continuing with his lessons in anatomy, Mather reminds his reader that "in the *Body* of Man there is nothing deficient, nothing superfluous, and *End* and *Use* for every thing"

(p. 224), with "no sign of *Chance* in the whole Structure of our Body" (p. 225). He finds much to praise, even trying to approach his subject aesthetically: "What can be more *ornamental*, than that those Members which are in *Pairs*, do stand by one another in an *equal Altitude*" (p. 226).

Still considering the body as a whole, Mather is impressed by the provision made for the body to "*stave off Evils*" (p. 226). A paragraph follows on the ways the body can rid itself of "mischiefs" and whatever is offensive to it. Next to be considered is the "*Harmony* and *Sympathy* between the Members of the Body" (p. 227). Our nerves, muscles, and glands are so contrived that our faces show our emotion—and walking on a cold floor will cause bellyache: "What a Sympathy between the *Feet* and the *Bowels!*" (p. 228). Another part of God's providence for man is to be seen in "three Remarkable *Dissimilitudes* between *Men* and *Men*," no two being alike in their faces, voices, and handwritings (p. 228).

After briefly noting the "variety of the parts" that compose the body (bones, muscles, nerves, skin) and then the "variety of offices" which each part performs (the tongue and diaphragm, by way of illustration, functioning in more than one way), Mather almost loses his organization in considering the difficult subjects of pain and sleep. But after digressing to these more general topics, he decides to examine particular parts of the body.

Making the obvious choice, he starts with the head. The nerves, brain, and hair hold his attention only briefly, although he returns to the nerves and brain from time to time in subsequent discussions. Most "marvelous and curious" is the eye, with nine pages (pp. 235 - 44) devoted to its construction. Next comes a fairly detailed account of the anatomy of the ear, followed by a discussion of sound. This leads to the senses other than hearing: smelling, tasting, and feeling, all considered briefly (pp. 253 - 55), but he takes time to comment that seeing, hearing, smelling, and tasting have their "*peculiar Seats*," but feeling is "dispersed thro the whole Body, both without and within." Furthermore, "the *Organ* of this wonderful Sense, is the *Nerves*; which are, in a most curious, astonishing, incomparable manner, scattered throughout the whole Body" (p. 255).

Mather then found himself "pretty near" the teeth (pp. 255 - 57); soon he is exclaiming about the tongue, the "main Organ of Tasting" where "the Spittle has its Vent," but whose "grand Glory" is that it is the "main Instrument of speaking" (pp. 257 - 58). Passing "down from the Mouth," he comments on the structure of the windpipe, gullet, and glottis (pp. 259 - 61), cites a number of authorities on respiration (and its relation to blood circulation), and admires the lungs, "a most surprising Piece of Workmanship," that inflate at birth (pp. 261 - 64). The "Divine Workmanship about the Heart" includes not only arteries, veins, and valves, but also the relation of the heart and brain (pp. 264 - 66).

As he continues describing the organs of man's body, Mather has one favorite word: admirable. He praises the stomach for the wonders of digestion (pp. 266 - 68), the intestines for keeping their "tone" and "site" for scores of years as they give an "undisturbed Passage to what every day passes thro them" (pp. 268 - 69); the liver, which does "admirable things, in continually separating the *Choler* from the Blood, and emptying it into the *Intestines*, where it is useful"; the bladder, an "admirable Vessel," with its ureters; and how admirable the kidneys, with their "little and curious Tubes" acting as siphons (p. 269).

Having thus commented on the wonders of the functioning of specific organs, Mather returns to the body in general. Although each of the glands is "an admirable Congeries of many Vessels" (p. 270), he contents himself with recommending in a brief paragraph that his reader consult suggested authorities on the subject. The bones, joints, and muscles show their admirable attributes more comprehensibly (pp. 270 - 71). As still another part of God's wisdom in planning man's body, there is no "unnecessary Vacuity" in it, but every part is "clothed, joined, corroborated by *Membranes*," the organs are "involved in" coats, and the whole is kept warm by fat (p. 274). The *"Spirits in Man"* are fetched out of the blood by the *"Laboratory* of the *Brain"* (p. 275). Under blood, too, he considers, albeit briefly, the "marvelous" lymph system (pp. 275 - 76).

Finally, somewhat anticlimactically, Mather almost ceases to be the scientist as he has as his last lesson in anatomy the hand—the hand which is writing this book and which is the "handy-work of our God." He has surprisingly little to say, however, about the actual structure of the hand; instead he offers a number of examples of prodigious strength (pp. 277 - 81).

Much as he apparently enjoyed proving both his knowledge of science in general and especially his reading in anatomy and medical theory, Mather brought himself back in the last twenty-odd pages of *The Christian Philosopher* to his avowed purpose: his natural philosophy, as he said, terminating in theology. He managed, moreover, in his discussion of the soul to follow the same basic pattern that he had used for the body and for all his other essays, an approach through reason to faith; that is, he begins by treating more or less demonstrable attributes, then makes his religious application. In other words, the reader is first asked to admire the "stupendous Faculties" of the soul—faculties that include wisdom, reason, learning, memory, and invention. In this discussion Mather uses "soul" in the broader sense of man's animating principle that includes the faculty of thought, much as "mind" is commonly used today; he omits the question of emotion. (In the religious application that follows he uses "soul" in a theological sense, as man's spiritual nature in relation to God.)

If wisdom is the first of these faculties that impresses Mather, as a Calvinist minister he quickly interrupts himself to say that the Love of God in the soul or the "principle of Grace infused in it" is more noble than all other faculties (p. 282).

Reason, the second of man's inherent powers, is clearly defined as "a *Faculty* formed by God, in the Mind of Man, enabling him to discern certain *Maxims of Truth*, which God himself has established" (p. 283). And as the Voice of God is in the "Dictates of Reason," man must comply with these dictates in all points from mathematics to morality. He cites a few simple examples of unarguable facts in mathematics, but he offers no examples of moral questions that can be resolved by reason.

On the other hand, Mather is generous with examples to illustrate the faculty of learning. He praises a number of earlier theologians and scholars that he particularly admired, including Usher,[3] Grotius,[4] Alsted,[5] Witsius,[6] and Baxter.[7] If the achievements of youthful scholars are especially noteworthy, the scholarly attainments of blind preachers, writers, and teachers are even more remarkable; again he cites examples. For the faculty of memory, too, Mather names many outstanding possessors of this ability, from Seneca to his own contemporaries.

With the last faculty, invention, a different approach is apparent: "things of *greater* use were *sooner* invented, things of a *lesser* use *later*" (p. 289). Here Mather, showing his scientific turn of thought, is obviously more interested in the accomplishment than in the man or men behind it as he reports that printing was developed in 1430, the telescope in 1609, the science of anatomy in his own day. After a longish consideration of man's progress from sundials to clocks and then a short note on the progress that mathematics seemed to be making, Mather leaves man's individual faculties as he finds himself "soaring into the *invisible World*, a World of *Intellectual Beings*" (p. 292).

All his life Cotton Mather, like most of his contemporaries, was a firm believer in angels; to doubt the existence of angels was to question the veracity of the Bible. His *Diary* frequently records his ecstatic confidence that he is being assisted in his preaching or writing or doing good by the "Angelical Ministry"; during more personal crises he tells, in a paroxysm of intense faith, that it is his "own Angel" that makes a "lustrous descent" into his study. In *The Christian Philosopher*, however, Mather is much more objective: the reader is informed that the belief in angels should be not only a matter of faith but also of reason; he then bases his whole proof of the existence of these spiritual beings on reason, arguing from the Chain of Being theory.

The concept of a Chain of Being or Scale of Nature is as old as Plato and Aristotle, but it gained new prominence among educated men in the seventeenth and eighteenth centuries. Leibnitz, Locke, and Addison are perhaps the best-known thinkers contemporary with Cotton Mather who expounded upon the idea, but belief in it was common among natural philosophers and scientists as early as Sir Francis Bacon and as late as the end of the eighteenth century.[8] According to Mather's interpretation and use of the Scale of Nature, "as we pass regularly and proportionably from a Stone to a Man" the "Faculties of the Creatures" grow brighter and more capacious until we arrive at Man, who is "*but the Equator of the Universe*" (p. 293). The reason for man's mid position is:

It is likely that the Transition from *Human* to *perfect* MIND is made by a *gradual Ascent;* there may be *Angels* whose Faculties may be as much superior to *ours*, as ours may be to those of a *Snail* or a *Worm* (p. 293).

These "perfect" and "excellent" minds, "divested of all Body," can possess knowledge by "immediate Intuition" and are without "Inclination to any *moral Evil*." Finally, the highest perfection in any created mind is in the soul of the Savior, or rather, in the soul of the man who is personally united to the Son of God (p. 293).

Thus Mather comes to his conclusion: atheism is forever "chased and hissed out of the World" (p. 294). The work of God proves that there is a God; nor is the Savior to be forgotten, for he has ever had the "natural Government of the World" (p. 302). With the thought of Christ, Mather is led to contemplate the joys of His chosen people in their future state. His prayer for himself has Pauline echoes but it is also in the spirit of the Chain of Being enthusiasts: *"Lord, I hope for an eternally progressive Knowledge, from the Lamb of God successively leading me to the Fountains of it!"* (p. 303).

Having reached this grand philosophical and theological finale on the relationship of man and his Creator, Mather—as in so many of his publications—cannot resist one last point. He returns to his often-expressed claim that reason supports religion as he offers his reader a "low" explanation, taken from his respected Cheyne, of the Trinity. The explication is "low" because it attempts a clarification of the Trinity by reason when man traditionally should accept this doctrine by faith; nevertheless, Mather felt that he had to include a philosophical hypothesis suggesting that even this "incomprehensible Mystery" could be bolstered by reason. Intelligent beings, he argues, have their whole being in three principles: the Desire, the Object, and the Sensation. The archetype of this division may be found in the Godhead, for Desire may be "apprehended" in God the Father; the only fit object of His desire for happiness is God the Son; the Love and Joy with which God contemplates the Son (Who is God) is the Holy Spirit (pp. 303 - 304).

And now the assiduous author is satisfied that he has finished his proof of the happy relationship between reason and faith, science and religion. As he says, somewhat triumphantly, "But it is time to stop here, and indeed how can we go any further!" (p. 304).

His feeling of accomplishment was indeed justified. Considering the difficulties of his subject, he had produced a lively and readable book. Although he quotes and paraphrases steadily, he manages his material well. Perhaps most important, he chose his points or proofs well—they still often are of genuine interest; modern scientists also note that he chose wisely in the sense that later developments in science frequently have shown the correctness of many of his statements concerning both scientific facts and theories.[9] Most obviously, his intelligent selection of authorities is indicated by his respectful devotion to Newton's ideas; not only does he cite "the incomparable Sir Isaac Newton" directly, but many of his other authorities also had been strongly influenced by Newtonian concepts. *The Christian Philosopher*, especially in its first eleven essays on astronomical subjects, shows, in fact, the first extensive use of Newtonian science in America.

Then, too, his style is clear and direct, with difficult or muddy paragraphs very much the exception. In contrast to his earlier practice, he offers his reader no nuggets of wisdom that do not bear directly upon his subject. Nor does he often wander from his main intent; even his tirade against tobacco and smoking (pp. 135 - 36), a topic about which he felt strongly and wrote frequently, is an understandable digression in a study that has to say so much about man's body.

One of the most pleasing qualities of the book is its author's enthusiasm.[10] He succeeds in convincing his reader that thinking about his subject was a constant pleasure. His religious fervor is to be expected as it is present in all his writing, from the most personal entry in his *Diary* to every instructional or historical essay he produced. In this book, however, he also seems to have attained a scientific spirit, with the intricate construction of an insect or of a human eye giving him real satisfaction.

Even more attractive is Mather's enjoyment of nature. He rejoices in the "Gaiety and Fragrancy" of flowers, with their "luxuriant Colours" (p. 127); he admires the bee as an "exquisite Chymist" (p. 153); he is glad that waterfowl have long legs "naked a good way above the knees" (p. 180) to aid in their wading. He seems sympathetic with the fondness of seals for their young (p. 178) and with the care that birds take of their fledglings (p. 194). At times he even approaches identification with nature when he sees the moon "walking in her Brightness" (p. 47) or comments that birds "invite us to *soar* and *sing* with them in the Praises of our God" (p. 180). If Mather is still a far way from the Transcendentalism of the nineteenth century, at least he prepares the student of American literature for the Emerson that is to come.

Considered in the general context of the history of thought, *The Christian Philosopher* is, then, both a readable summary of scientific thinking in the early eighteenth century and an indication of how men, not willing to abandon their religious tenets, would react to the new scientific knowledge about the universe that the Age of Reason was developing. Considered as a work of the mature years of its author, the book (together with the *Manuductio* of 1726) is evidence that Cotton Mather, faithful to Calvinism and nostalgic as he might be about the theocracy of New England's first years, adjusted with acumen and dignity to a changing world. Perhaps, as he hoped, he helped others in their reconciliation of science and religion. Certainly his own concept of his Creator and of Creation had been developed by his study of the new science.

CHAPTER 10

The Angel of Bethesda

To make myself more *useful* unto my Neighbours in their Afflictions; not only releeving the *Poor*, but also the *Sick;* to which purpose, I would collect, at Leisure a fit number of most parable[1] and effectual Remedies for all Diseases, and publish them unto the world; so, by my Hand will bee done things that the *Angels* love to do. (*Diary*, March 1693)

My large Work, entituled, THE ANGEL OF BETHESDA, is now finished. If my glorious Lord will please to accept of it, it may prove one of the most useful Books, that have been written in the World. I must now apply myself both to Heaven and Earth, to bring on the Publication of it. (*Diary*, February 1723/4)

THE book that Cotton Mather finally thought of as completed in 1724 (and struggled in vain to have published) was very much of an extension of his plans of 1693. *The Angel of Bethesda*[2] is no ordinary herbal or pharmacopoeia or manual of medicine. Faced with illness in her family, a busy housewife might have checked in it for possible remedies; other parts of this "most useful" book, however, seem to be meant for educated readers willing to consider scientific and philosophical questions. But by missing its audience of 1724, the result of Mather's diligent labors was fated to be of use neither medically nor, as he hoped with equal fervor, spiritually.

The author's interest in medicine started early—according to his own account, when he was eleven, a student at Harvard, and realized that his stammer might keep him from following his family's tradition of preaching. The alleviation of his speech difficulty did not end his pursuit of medical lore, and throughout his life he read whatever books and treatises he could acquire or borrow. Although he did not start actually writing the *Angel* for many years after his resolve of 1693, he made use of his medical reading in a number of other publications, most notably in his *Curiosa Americana* (1712 -

1724) and *The Christian Philosopher* (completed in 1715, published in 1721). Then, after he had completed *The Christian Philosopher* but while he was still contributing material to the Royal Society, apparently sometime between 1718 and 1720, he commenced to put the long-delayed *Angel of Bethesda* into form; by the first months of 1724 he considered it ready for the press.

Despite his lifelong interest in medicine, Cotton Mather did not look upon himself as a doctor, nor did he in any sense practice medicine. In the frequent illness of his family and of himself, he called in local practitioners. When discussing in the *Angel of Bethesda* serious illnesses that might be fatal, such as smallpox, he stresses the very urgent need of having an experienced doctor watch the course of the disease to adjust the treatment and nursing care to the patient's condition.

On the other hand, he could see nothing untoward in his extended "good deed" of helping the sick by writing such a book as the *Angel*. Quite rightly, he believed that he was a well-read man, accustomed to spending many hours each day in studying, and one who not only had the best library in New England to draw upon but who also kept abreast of the latest theories in all fields of science through the *Transactions* of the Royal Society and its German counterpart, the *Ephemeridum Medico-Physicarum*. Like other scholars of his period, he did not see knowledge as departmentalized; an educated man was at home in the various fields of what was called natural philosophy, including chemistry and medicine.

In considering Cotton Mather's temerity in composing a book of medical advice, it should also be remember that few of his contemporaries who made their living by medicine had any training that was at all professional in our modern sense. Most colonial practitioners read whatever medical books were available, perhaps served as an apprentice to an older doctor for three years or less, and then considered themselves qualified to begin treating patients. And even these doubtfully qualified doctors were in short supply in the colonies. At the time of the 1721 epidemic of smallpox in Boston, the population of the city is calculated to have been about 11,000 (before the exodus of those able to leave), with only ten to twelve doctors available; only one of the latter had any sort of medical degree.[3]

The Angel of Bethesda patently was not meant to be considered an original treatise on medicine. On the contrary, its author makes a proud parade of his learning, repeatedly giving his sources. He goes back to the old authorities, Hippocrated, Galen, Paracelsus, even citing Zoroaster and Plato (and the Platonic school); but more frequently he is showing his respectful familiarity with the men of the new science, van Helmont, Boyle, Sydenham—name after name, book after book. All told, he cites some 250 philosophers and scientists. When he reaches the body of the book and is listing numerous possible remedies for specific diseases and pathological condidtions, many of his suggestions are folk medicine; for these, of course, he can give no scholarly authority unless, as was true of more than one-third of the remedies, he had seen them reported in print.

Nor does the *Angel* make any pretense of offering only freshly written material. Cotton Mather, following his usual method in composing books of any length, drew heavily upon whatever he thought applicable in his earlier publications: a number of sermons, the chapter on physicians in his *Bonifacius*, the physiological section of *The Christian Philosopher*, some of his pamphlets on the smallpox controversy of 1721, letters that he had written to the Rpyal Society, even a personal item (on stammering) from his *Diary*. The subject matter in each case makes its inclusion justifiable, but in this volume of short chapters and of succinct items within each chapter these reprintings tend to break the tone and pace of the book.

By December of 1720, when he was actually in the process of organizing and writing the *Angel of Bethesda*, Cotton Mather had decided to devote a short chapter or, in his wording, a "Capsula," to each disease; each time he would first "offer the sentiments of piety which the ditempered are thereby the most naturally, and rationally and religiously, to be led unto" and then subjoin "such powerful and parable specifics as in my reading or otherwise I have met withal"[4] for the cure of the malady. This prosaic, practical plan was his overall intent, but, as was his custom in writing his longer works, he felt the necessity of an impressive introduction. And having reached his undertaking as planned—that is, to give for each disease the correct interpretation of the suffering involved, then offer possible cures for the ailment—Mather also was too much of an individualist to pursue a set pattern without allowing himself an occasional insertion of apropos material or discussion. Finally, with the last capsulas, any pattern is simply abandoned.

I   Introductory Chapters: Causes of Disease: Psychosomatic Medicine: Animaculae—The Germ Theory

The Angel of Bethesda starts with the question that men have raised in all ages: "Why is there disease and suffering?" or the more perplexing cry of anguish, "Why does a good God permit disease and suffering?" In answering Mather uses dogma that most Christians and all Calvinists of his day fully accepted. Sin is the cause of disease; evil came into the world with the fall of Adam and Eve; man continues to sin and so by suffering is both punished for his sins, past and current, and warned against future sinning. The suffering of children, apparently so unfairly cruel, may well be due to the sins of the parents. (Mather in these first chapters is very much the clergyman reiterating doctrine that his parishioners had heard periodically from the Old North pulpit.)[5]

Nevertheless, despite the Fall, a kindly God has provided in nature anodynes for man's pain—if man is properly penitent and prayerful. In Christ is the forgiveness of sin; therefore man must turn to Jesus as "The Lord our Healer," for the health of the soul is all important. As for man's bodily well-being, abstemiousness or moderation in all the physical aspects of life is the fundamental rule.

Man should read the Bible, for the Word of God is the most wholesome food, and he should pray. His giving of alms to the poor (as a sign of obedience to God's will) will make his prayers more easily heard. Here Cotton Mather is back to his often-repeated plea for everyone to be good, to be charitable.

Then, temporarily deserting the standard theology and instruction of many years of pulpit oratory, Cotton Mather in his fifth capsula, "Nismath-Chajim. The probable Seat of all Diseases, and a general Cure for them, further discussed" (28 - 37), raises philosophical, psychological, and biological questions that have continuing interest. This is the one chapter of the book that Mather succeeded in having printed, in 1722, presumably through the generosity of his Connecticut friend John Winthrop.[6] Most probably, both author and patron decided that this chapter was an impressive sampling of the projected book, for in its first pages Mather really is giving a history of an old philosophic hypothesis on the relationship of the body and the soul (or mind), with a postulated intermediary between them.[7] Few writers other than Mather would have attempted to cover the subject in a short essay meant for lay readers.

According to Mather's argument, the Nismath-Chajim is the spirit of man, literally the "Breath of Life," of a "Middle Nature between the Rational Soul, and the Corporeal Mass," the Medium of Communication" between Body and Soul. To convince his readers of the existence of the Nismath-Chajim, every authority in whom Mather could find a "suspicion" or a "Whif" or a "Notion" or a "Scent" of the idea is cited, from Plato to van Helmont, the seventeenth-century mystic (as well as physicist and chemist). The Nishmath-Chajim is our strength and our "Main Digester," but also the source of our diseases. (Many men of the period believed that the stomach was the seat of all man's physical troubles, or in Mather's phraseology, the "Grand Wheel in the Machine.")

With this development of the theory, Cotton Mather has reached the basic concepts of psychosomatic medicine: it is through "Heaviness in the Heart of Man" or "Weight of Cares" that many of our illnesses come; it is through "Tranquility of Mind," or "Expectation" or "Bright Thoughts" that cure comes. Some anodynes can be given to the sufferer for temporary relief; exercise will help; but, above all, "Serious Piety" is the remedy.

After this masterful attempt at explaining the influence of the mind or soul on the health of the body, Cotton Mather, as if exhausted by his efforts, drops (in the sixth capsula) to a somewhat commonplace, even lighthearted discourse on the value of exercise. "Chafing" (massage) and walking can be helpful, but "the Saddle is the Seat of Health," except in a case of too thin blood or of "feminine difficulties" (42).

But with the seventh capsula the earnest author is offering his reader recent and exciting discoveries. In "Conjecturalies or, Some Touches upon, A New Theory of many Diseases" (43 - 48) Mather is at his best, combining the enthusiasm of having a new concept of the physical world opened to him and a prompt realization of the application of this new knowledge to the prevention of disease. With the invention of the microscope in the late sixteenth century and its improvement in the seventeenth, the field of microscopy developed. For the first time scientists became aware of the "animalculae" that surround man. In Mather's vivid words:

Every part of Matter is *Peopled*. Every *Green Leaf* swarms with *Inhabitants*. The surfaces of Animals are covered with other *Animals*. Yes, the most solid *Bodies*, even *Marble* itself, have innumerable Cells, which are crouded with imperceptible Inmates. As there are Infinite Numbers of these, which the *Microscopes* bring to our View, so there may be in-

conceivable Myriads yett Smaller than these, which no glasses have yett
reach'd unto. The *Animals* that are much *more* than Thousands of times
Less than the finest Grain of Sand, have their motions. . . .

Mather quickly grasped the hypothesis that in pathogenic
animalculae (in modern lay speech, "germs") the cause of disease
could be found:

The Eggs of thsee Insects (and why not the *Living Insects* too!) may in-
sinuate themselves by the Air, . . . yea, thro' the Pores of our skin; and
soon get into the juices of our Bodies.

Going one step further, he suggests the possible cause of congenital
disease:

They [the animalculae] may be convey'd into our Fluids, with the *Nourish-
ment* which we received, even before we were born; and may ly dormant
until the Vessels are grown more capable of bringing them into their Figure
and Vigour for Operations. Thus may Disease be convey'd from the Parents
unto their Children, before they are born into the world (43 - 44).

He also cites various European authorities who were certain that
they had seen (with the aid of their microscopes) the "animals" in
ulcers, cancers, pustules of smallpox, blood, and urine. Nor does he
neglect to note that animalculae carried in the bodies or clothes of
travelers could be the cause of epidemics and plagues.

In none of this reporting and theorizing was Cotton Mather
breaking new ground. He refers to a dozen men before him who
had found the animalculae and then connected the discovery with
various diseases and malignancies. From the points that he made,
Mather obviously had read a recent book, Benjamin Marten's *A
New Theory of Consumption*, a London publication of 1720; but he
also had made himself familiar—perhaps through Marten, but in
some cases certainly through their own publications—with the work
of other noted microscopists, including the renowned Antony van
Leewenhoek (1632 - 1723).

It is impossible to know what would have happened in the
development of American medicine if the *Angel* had reached print
in the first half of the eighteenth century, but presumably very little; almost certainly the animalculae hypothesis, advanced by a
layman and buried as it is in a collection of empirical remedies and
religious homilies, would not have impressed medical men. We do

know that the book failed of publication and that for many years American scientists and doctors made no use of discoveries through microscopy. It was not until the early nineteenth century that there was a rebirth of interest; this faded out, and it was only during the last quarter of the century, after the work of Lister and Pasteur, that the bacteriological approach to the prevention of disease was completely recognized by the medical profession.

As the seventh capsula, with its willingness to accept new scientific concepts, is in sharp contrast to the preceding one, so the eighth is surprising after the seventh. Capsula VIII, "Raphael. Or Notable Cures, from the Invisible World" (48 - 54), is just what its caption indicates: a series of cures accomplished by following advice given in dreams or gained by really sincere prayer; such cures Mather believed to be demonstrations of the Ministry of Good Angels.

II *Specific Diseases and Cures*

With the ninth chapter Mather starts on his plan of devoting short chapters to separate diseases, with the moral to be drawn from the suffering involved, followed by possible cures for the affliction. Having started, he uses the same pattern forty-four times,[8] only occasionally abbreviating the introductory religious sentiments and warnings, as in Capsula LX, on "Cures and Helps for a Cluster of Lesser Inconveniences" (279 - 286), which he regarded as a supplement.

"Dentifrangibulus. Or, The Anguish, and Relief, of the Toothache" (61 - 66), the eleventh of the book's sixty-two capsulas, is typical of Mather's labors, although a bit more personal than some of the sections as the author often had to endure periods of toothache and obviously yearned for both sympathy and relief. Consequently, he approaches the problem with marked despondency: Everyone is doomed to have "Fifty-two Tormentors" in his gums (including the first twenty milk teeth). But Mather quickly recovers himself, and, aware of his duty to instruct, gives a short lecture on the structure of human teeth. On reaching his next point, the "sentiments of piety" called for, Mather, always the inveterate punster whether suffering or not, cannot resist offering them as "truths to be chew'd upon": the sin of Adam and Eve was perpetuated by their teeth; men use their teeth to sin in overeating; men use their teeth in "speaking amiss." If the pains of toothache seem intolerable, think of the pains of damnation. Think, too, as you see your perishing teeth "agoing," that you are "agoing after them," or approaching death.

After thus putting his reader in the proper religious frame of mind, he offers some general prophylactic advice about the good effects of washing the teeth and behind the ears every day with cold water. Now he is ready to give the possible remedies for toothache (a malady which he feels physicians do not take seriously enough). There are eighteen suggestions for relieving pain, starting with "Thrust the Eye of a Needle into the Bowels of a *Sow-Bug;* and the Matter which it fetches out, putt in the *Hollow* Tooth, and ending with palliatives somewhat better known today, oil of cloves and the application of heat. Alas, none of these eagerly collected possibilities may be effective; then, "If there's nothing else to be done, *Draw the Tooth!*"

Some of the capsulas devoted to specific sicknesses are even shorter than "Dentifrangibulus," some a page or two longer. Almost all give an effect of terseness, as if the author had so many points to make that he could not linger over them. Occasionally, however, this pattern of brief chapters is broken by such inclusions as an old sermon on preparation for childbirth. With some humor, he also deliberately allows his essay on gout to be a "swol'n article" of thirteen pages: sufferers from this misfortune usually would be educated and wealthy, and so have time to read (and appreciate the knowledge and wit displayed).

The homilies that start each capsula are brief and forceful. If they do not move twentieth-century readers, they do demonstrate the ingenuity of seventeenth-century preaching. Churchgoers in colonial New England were accustomed to hearing sermons with many points driven home by apt comparisons with the human body and its illnesses. Insensitivity to sin was to be thought of by the congregation as lethargy, contention within the church as fever, hypocrites as abnormal growths or wens that sap the strength of the body. In the *Angel*, Cotton Mather simply uses a type of inverse similitude (as those metaphors and similes used in sermons were then named), starting with the physical and proceeding to the religious point: the fall of the epileptic is symbolic of the fall of the soul into sin; vertigo or dizziness should bring to mind the "giddy soul" staggering in its faith; if you pity the madman, how much more you should pity the man mad enough to reject Christ.

The cures are offered, rapidly, often in a line or two, and in no apparent order. For example, to help the sufferer from asthma he suggests as beneficial calmness of mind, a gentle vomit, bleeding, diuretics, "gum ammoniacum" in hyssop water and vine, balsam of sulphur, cow's urine (either undiluted or in beer), mustard seed, elecampane made into a syrup with rum or brandy, horehound, powdered eggshells, saffron, water gruel, "spirit of Tobacco . . . the most Specific Remedy in the World against this Disease," and applications of "spirituous and Castorine Medicines" (178 - 179).

In the course of giving hundreds of possible ways of treating disease, Mather questions the rationale or the efficiency of only a very few. He does doubt the wisdom of vinegar as a reducing diet; and he wonders why the milk with which urine is to be mixed has to come from a red cow. He also reports himself as being "slow to advise the giving of *Lice* . . . in the Jaundice," not only because of patient objections; he has also read of sad aftermaths of the practice. More frequently, however, he is satisfied to suggest an anodyne but give it scant recommendation: so in cures for dropsy, "an Ounce of the syrup of Buck-thorn, may do well" and "a Vomit may not be amiss, if the Stomach heave that Way"; as to sow-bug wine, "the Learned assure us, This is an admirable Medicine" (127).

On the other hand, Cotton Mather evinces great confidence in many of his cures; for example, the reader is told with great positiveness that "the Blood of an Ass,[9] drawn from behind his Ear, has a Singular and Wonderful Vertue, in destroying the *Volatil Acid*, which is the Cause of *Madness*" (131). The most enthusiastic capsula of all is "The Breast-beater, or, A Cough quieted" (172 - 176), with many anodynes that he has actually tried. If the cures are mostly gentle examples of natural or folk medicine (horehound, honey, liquorice, conserve of roses, barley jelly), Cotton's gratitude for many of them has a curious touch of modern advertising: efficacious "beyond all Imagination," "strikes at the Root" (castile soap in wine or beer), "hardly to be parallel'd," "good, safe, marvellous," "can't be too much commended," "notable," "infallible," "matchless"; in fact, the midnight cougher, poor wounded "nightingale," could scarcely avoid being cured.

Having decided to do his prolonged good deed of helping the sick, Cotton Mather seems to labor compulsively to include all the cures he can find, even ones that are, as he recognizes, white magic or the work of the Devil and his cohorts. Furthermore, after such a tale of a reported cure, he questions whether good men should use it, for they may find "such *Remedies* worse than the *Diseases* they are used for." In an item longer than his usual remedies, he cites a case (as related by "honest Philip Woodman") of a man who, troubled by stones in his bladder, buried his urine in three stone crocks; six months later, when presumably the urine had evaporated, he was cured (87). Or, with even less hesitation, Mather provides a "Magnetical Cure" in which a man rids himself of jaundice by putting a few drops of his urine in a sheep's gall bladder, which he then hangs up to dry (195). Perhaps because this cure came from the respected Robert Boyle's "receits," Mather attaches no warning to it.

Nor does Mather hesitate to offer remedies with ingredients that would be difficult for the average patient or his family to obtain: flour of brimstone (sulphur), vitriol (copper sulphate), terra sigillata (aluminous earth found in Lemnos), olibanum (frankincense), balsam of copeyba (copaiba, a resin of a West Indian tree) are typical constituents of many of the receipts that the deligent compiler had come upon. And even the most efficient housewife in colonial New England might not have in her cupboard the pizzle (penis) of a turtle, peacock dung, the thigh-bone of a toad, powdered crab eyes, red blisters found on oyster shells, and the oil of foxes—to name but a few of the demands that could be made upon her when sickness came into her family. Of course, if she were sufficiently strong of stomach, she might have been able to produce a mouse "flay'd and dried in a warm oven and powder'd" for anyone who had the misfortune to be incontinent.

It is not until Mather reaches his fifty-fourth capsula that he reminds himself that he is writing not only for the sick, but for the poor and sick, the families of limited ability to secure many of the ingredients that his cures as often as not called for. Although he indignantly denies that his *Angel* has more than a few "Tedious and Laboured Compositions," he suddenly shifts from his listing of all possible remedies that he has found in his long years of reading; the next five chapters are devoted to the "mean things" that all can use in their self-doctoring.

"Great Things done by Small Means" (248 - 252) extols the curative powers of animal and human excrement;[10] the next capsula, "More, great Friends to Health, very Easy to come at" (253 - 256), distinguishes the diffrent uses of warm beer, strong beer, small beer, and beer with wine "incorporated with it." There are even more easily obtained aids at hand: water (especially water boiled in

an iron vessel and allowed to stand in it, a "Universal Medicine")
and milk. He then leaves oral cures completely to consider the
beneficial effects of stroking with a dead hand, "out of measure
wonderful." The next capsula returns to more ordinary household
remedies: bread, both chewed and as a poultice, and water—this
time cold water, including cold baths.

With his fourth chapter of helpful suggestions Mather asks his
reader to remember another type of cure. "A Physick-Garden"
(262 - 269) describes a number of useful herbs, but Mather soon
leaves the garden to consider the valuable properties of oil of
almonds (for which whale oil can be substituted) and then "adds a
word" about apples and apple juice. But he returns to herbs: the
general method of use is to hang the herbs in fermenting li-
quor—wine, ale, beer, or cider. He can then boldly affirm that
"there is Scarcely any Chronical Disease, that is cured by the Shop-
medicines, which may not be cured with more Certainty, Ease, and
Pleasure, by Drinks thus ordered, joined with a Regular Diet" (268).

With all these helpful possibilities, Cotton Mather is not quite
through offering cures that are easily attainable or at least have a
humble source. In one more capsula, "Thaumatographia Insec-
torum. or, Some Despicable Insects of Admirable Vertues" (269 -
271), he decides to "call in" three insects: the bee with its honey of
use in many medicines; millipedes or sow-bugs, with "more *Virtues*,
than their Name does assign *Feet* unto them"; and Spanish flies,
whose bodies supply cantharides, a strong but most useful oint-
ment, especially for blistering, and if some doctors think it
dangerously strong, it is a very safe rat poison.

After these five chapters devoted to natural medicine, Mather
returns for a few more chapters to his regular pattern of giving the
moral uses and the possible cures of individual diseases. This
pattern has not been completely monotonous, however, for he has
broken the series by adding appendixes whenever he felt more information or new discoveries would help his readers. Thus the capsula on kidney stones has an appendix on other urinary diseases; the
one on epilepsy is followed by a new and supposedly infallible cure
(mistletoe) for children's convulsions.[11] Nor is he always satisfied
with one appendix. In an additional chapter (287 - 293) of advice to
the ordinary householder (inserted after he had completed his capsulas on separate diseases), instruction on how to make poultices
leads into a defense of gentlewomen who help their poor neighbors
with simple remedies;[12] but the appendix proper, so labeled, is a

short but interesting consideration of simple preventives for oc-
cupational diseases;[13] this in turn is followed by a collection of easy
emetics and then of easy cathartics.

Capsula XXXIX (179 - 186) on consumption (tuberculosis) has a
certain poignancy since Cotton Mather's much loved daughter Katy
had died in 1716, a victim of this common scourge of the time. Even
as he prepared her for death, the fond father had, with many days
of fasting and prayer, struggled to save her, to find some way of easing her suffering. It is after this capsula that the author feels that he
should insert a summary (with brief illustrative quotations) of the
startling contradictions he had found in medical treatises on the
best treatment for consumptive patients. If he had followed his
usual method of handling his material, this essay would have been
appended to the previous chapter, but "A Pause made upon, The
Uncertainties of the physicians" (186 - 191) is separately captioned
as Capsula XL. He shows no bitterness, no contempt for doctors;
they are often sorely needed. Nevertheless, the lesson is that man
should depend on God, not on any "arm of Flesh."

III   *Inoculation against Smallpox: The Beginning of Immunology*

All the appendixes in the *Angel* are of interest, often of more interest than the chapters themselves; in fact, it is the appendix to the
chapter on smallpox that modern medical historians praise as a
recording of Cotton Mather's outstanding contribution to
prophylactic medicine and as the most valuable part of his whole
ambitious book. The chapter itself, Capsula XX, explains in detail
the currently preferred treatment in smallpox cases: keeping the
patient at different stages warm or cool, the use of narcotics, the
proper liquids. In all this advice Mather is obviously dependent on
"my" and "our" Sydenham, the most respected seventeenth-
century authority on bedside care, although he carefully adds
suggestions by other authorities.

After this capsula, with its longer than usual religious introduction (smallpox as a particularly loathsome disease, very frequently
fatal, could be used in many ways to bring the patient—or the
reader—to a properly humble mind) and with its detailed instructions from the best authorities for easing the patient's suffering,
perhaps even keeping him alive, Mather suddenly announces that
he has a "further Story" to tell and that "hundreds of Thousands of
Lives will soon be Saved if my Story may be harken'd to." The

Appendix (107116) then recounts briefly and modestly his two-part "story": the practice of inoculation in other parts of the world and the introduction of this life-saving treatment into American medicine.

From a strictly medical viewpoint, the rest of the *Angel,* with the exception of the author's early recognition of the animalcular or germ theory as the cause of disease, is largely medieval lore that persistently dominated medical thinking as late as the eighteenth century (and in certain fields much later). But Mather's 1721 success in forcing the use of inoculation in Boston is the beginning of immunology, one of the most important and fundamental developments in modern medicine. It is ironic that this advance in medical practice was made through the knowledge and courage of Cotton Mather, who has long been thought of as an extremely credulous, would-be scientist. It also should be noted that he had the backing of his fellow Boston ministers, including his aged father, all men who might be stereotyped as accepting God's will in visiting His people with devastating plagues. On the other hand, the local doctors, with two praiseworthy exceptions, fought against the innovation, unwilling to accept what was to them a new idea if it came from nonprofessional sources.

With the modern interest in the history of medicine (and of all science), the introduction of inoculation into American medicine has been told a number of times and considered from many angles.[14] The tale need not be told again in detail, but there are a few salient facts to be kept in mind for any evaluation of Mather's efforts to have the practice initiated in Boston and observed by the rest of the English-speaking world.

First of all, his course of action in 1721 was not a sudden decision; as early as 1716 he had decided that it would be his duty in the next epidemic of smallpox to persuade the Boston doctors to start the practice of inoculating everyone who had not had the disease in previous epidemics. No disease brought more painful misery, more frequent deaths. Inoculation could end all this suffering, save many lives. He had originally learned about the common use of inoculation in Africa from his slave, Onesimus, and had then been told the same tale by other Africans in Boston. (It says much for Cotton Mather that in the early eighteenth century he listened to a slave and was willing to cite the African's story in all his defenses of the practice; the opponents of inoculation mocked him as a credulous minister willing to believe an ignorant slave's false or fanciful tale.)

But he did not depend solely on their oral accounts. In 1713 the first of two reports on the use of inoculation in Turkey appeared in the *Transactions* of the Royal Society,[15] and these reports were submitted by physicians of standing; there were also two other attesting statements by eyewitnesses.

Obviously, inoculation was being used successfully in other parts of the world. Mather's reading had also taught him that animalculae, apparently often the cause of disease, had been observed in the microscopic study of smallpox pustules. Unlike most of his contemporaries, who would have been satisfied with an empiric preventive, he developed a theory to explain why inoculation transmitted a light case of smallpox which had no ill effects but which gave the patient immunity from future attacks. According to Mather's reasoning,[16] when the animalculae entered the body by way of the lungs, the vital parts of the body were near and vulnerable. But by injecting the animalculae (from a pustule of someone having the disease) into the arm, the "appraches are made only by the *Outworks* of the Citadel, and the vital organs can throw off the infection.

Thus supported by authentic reports that inoculation had been in use for some time in other lands, by his knowledge of animalculae, and by his own hypothesis about the part the "little animals" played in the disease and its prevention, Cotton Mather was ready for the epidemic of 1721. As the disease became more and more rampant, he tried to persuade the doctors in Boston and the surrounding towns to hold "a consult" about stopping the epidemic by inoculation. They refused to respond, and so he persuaded the one medical man who would listern, Dr. Zabdiel Boylston, to carry out the experiment.

In spite of violent objections from many Bostonians and in spite of legal banning, the inoculations were performed with remarkable success. (The protests, which went so far as a bomb thrown into the Mather home, were based on a variety of claims: that there was danger involved in deliberately giving anyone smallpox, that such a preventive was unnatural and against God's will, and that inoculation would spread the epidemic rather than halt it.) Both Boylston and Mather were thankful that enough people were inoculated (242) to prove the safety of the new treatment; only six died, and most if not all of these deaths were from previous exposure to the disease or from other causes; if the same number of people had taken the disease in the usual way, there would have been thirty-five or more deaths.[17]

IV *Concluding Capsulas: Social, Religious Instruction*

Having told of the first successful use of inoculation in the English-speaking world, as an appendix to the twentieth chapter of a book of sixty-six chapters, Cotton Mather never returns to his accomplishment. He continues for disease after disease to give his moral points and his many cures culled from wherever he could find them. When he feels that he has covered all of men's illnesses, serious or only bothersome, he allows himself to express his very vehement feelings on a few matters.

The first part of Capsula LXII (293 - 301), one of Mather's letters to the Royal Society, is a protest against the use of charms to cure disease and against the old belief that a seventh son has special powers to cure disease. From ridiculing these types of superstition he slips easily into a tirade against the Catholic practice of appealing to various saints as having the power to cure certain ailments. Then, as a final type of foolish turning from true faith in God, he mentions contemptuously astrological beliefs, especially those to be found in Culpepper's popular manual.[18]

The following capsula, LXIII (301 - 11), is an emotional attack on the use of tobacco. The evils of smoking are many and frightening: not only is the flesh "Baconized" but "the *Memory* is impaired, the *Stomach* Violated, the *Brain* Exiccated, and the *Life* shortened"; and if smokers should live to have children, the latter are more than likely to be consumptive. But the horrors of smoking fade in comparison with the results of the disgusting habit of using snuff: the finer powder undoubtedly passes into the brain, ruining the eyes, stomach, and entire nervous system.

In both these chapters Mather is protesting as he had done many times previously against what he regarded as genuine social evils and signs of declining faith. The dependence on charms for health showed that men were turning to the Devil for help rather than to their Savior. The use of tobacco was a double sin as it undermined the body, the temple of the soul; and the indulgence in the habit showed that men no longer believed that all their thoughts and acts were for the service and glory of God. The bitter virulence of the attack in the *Angel* has, however, a very human explanation, and can be seen as an aftermath of the smallpox-inoculation controversy. Among the protestors against inoculation was an uneducated man by the name of John Williams, the local tobacconist, nicknamed Mundungus Williams (mundungus being an inferior, rank tobacco). This Mundungus, who was a firm believer in the value of charms, had written (presumably with the help of some better-educated Bostonians) a pamphlet attacking Cotton Mather and his advocacy of inoculation. The two chapters are Mather's indignant counterattack.

The short concluding chapters return to the religious instruction of the opening capsulas. Man should be properly thankful for recovery from illness; anyone who has lived a long life preserved from painful illness should indeed be thankful. Finally, in "Euthanasia. or, A Death Happy and Easy" (317 - 22), every man of good faith should accept death as going to a "Delectable World." But Cotton Mather, typically, has a good deed by which every man can be useful to the very end. Mindful of the standers-by at his deathbed, the dying man can "Lett fall some Solemn Words, useful Counsils, awful Charges, which it may be for the advantage of the Survivers, to remember all their Dayes."

V Cotton Mather's "Large" and "Most Useful" Book

Unlike Cotton Mather's other major works, *The Angel of Bethesda* leaves its reader somewhat confused—and with a strong suspicion that the author has overextended himself in this good deed. The basic conflict between faith and science (a conflict that Mather denied existed) is understandable: any man who believes in a good God has to say, "Thy will be done," but he then struggles against pain and death with all the knowledge he can command. As a Calvinist and a man of his time, the New England preacher resolved his dilemma triply by accepting that sinful man deserves to be punished, by believing that a kindly God gave man the means to help himself and therefore intended man to use this means, and by preaching again and again that nothing can be accomplished by man without prayer.

Even if these premises concerning faith and sickness are fully accepted, the coherence of the *Angel* is still a bothersome issue. At least part of the difficulty is that Cotton Mather does not carry through with what should be his most helpful theories. For example, he completely believes in the existence of animalculae and that they may be the cause of many diseases, but he returns to this theory only once, in his advocacy of inoculation. Again, he offers an elaborate hypothesis as an explanation of psychosomatic illness, tells the reader that many illnesses are psychosomatic, but ignores the whole question in his treatment of disease after disease, although he does admit once or twice that belief in a cure is the cure. (It is true that he treats insanity and melancholia through the body, but he does not seem to see this approach, the effect of the body on the mind, as the other side of the efffect of the mind on the body.)

Another difficulty with Mather's "most useful" book lies within the collections of cures contained in the capsulas devoted to separate diseases. It is, of course, indicative of ignorance of social and medical history to ridicule Cotton Mather for his cures, as they are not his creations, his ideas, but the medicine of his day, many of them coming from outstanding contemporary scientists and physicians. If there is fault to be found in Cotton Mather's faithful and largely uncritical listing of all these possible remedies, it is in their very number and variety, with many of them—even for the same disease—heartily recommended. He seems to be satisfied as long as he has found one more cure (even one through sympathetic or white magic) that someone knows about, very happy if it comes from a recognized scientist or physician. Is Mather unwilling to ignore any possibility that might be of benefit to the sick? Or is he parading his wide reading in old and new authorities? Whatever the author's motives or mixture of motives, which of the twenty or thirty (or more) cures is the "poor" and "sick" patient to settle upon?

The general organization of the *Angel* undoubtedly is weakened by the plethora of material that Cotton Mather offers: the eight introductory chapters that include two new (to America) theories of disease; the three sermonic concluding ones; the comprehensive survey of all the then-recognized diseases and conditions of ill health, with their many possible cures; the six capsulas supplying simple, natural cures commonly available and positively effective (thus making unnecessary all the other cures he has given); the scattered appendixes; the passionate capsulas of warning against the use of charms and the "lust for tobacco." Nevertheless, the book has clarity in the smaller sense. The instructions for the treatment of conditions needing extended care are easily understood, and the individual cures and anodynes are simply worded and terse. In other words, once the nurse or patient had selected which of the listed steps to recovery he preferred (or could attain), there would not have to be any hesitation about what Cotton Mather advised should be done.

The varied contents of the *Angel of Bethesda* clearly indicate that the author did not look upon his work only as a reference book to be consulted in sudden need but also kept in mind the more leisured audience he might hope to have.[19] Any contemporary, reading the *Angel* for the general benefit he might hope to derive from one of Mather's books, would have found that the steady fare of religious and medical instruction was happily broken from time to time by flashes of wit. Cotton Mather never neglected style; as he had said many years before, whatever his subject, he always tried to give his readers additional morsels of wisdom to be reflected upon. *The Angel of Bethesda* follows this theory of writing, but, presumably because of the seriousness and unpleasantness of so much of his material, the added bits are there as often as not to make his readers smile. The monotony of sickness and death is occasionally broken by an effective metaphor such as "Pride is the Dropsy of the Soul" (126). Or a piece of general wisdom is pleasantly, lightly worded: "*Every Man* is *Mad* in some *One Point*. . . . He is a very wise Man, who finds out his own *Mad Point*" (131).

One more virtue can be found in the *Angel of Bethesda*. If the author, toiling away at his "large" book, had hopes that his vast reading would be impressive, he might be surprised that it is his pervasive kindliness that is moving. In his *Diary* Mather is shown as a loving family man; here in the *Angel* it is good will toward much of mankind (always excepting Catholics and smokers!) that gently shines through. He really pities all who suffer and the poor little "pissabed" children; he would have the madman treated gently; he asks for patience with the melancholy, who can take far too much of a busy man's time and are the particular bane of ministers. If he is constantly urging the sick to prepare for death, he is being realistic, and it should be remembered that the preparation will insure a joyous hereafter. In the meantime, he seems genuinely happy in all the cures that God's bounty supplies and that he, Cotton Mather, poor worm but another (proud) Angel of Bethesda, can record.

CHAPTER 11

Manuductio ad Ministerium: Directions for a Candidate of the Ministry

THE idea of writing an "Enchiridion of the Liberal Sciences" had occurred to Cotton Mather as early as 1716,[1] but for some years he could not get around to this project, useful as he felt it would be. With the fading in 1724 of his chances of ever being president of Harvard and of refashioning the college according to his educational theories, he decided that he had no choice: the time had come to influence the younger generation by a comprehensive manual of this type. The result of his labors, the surprisingly readable *Manuductio ad Ministerium: Directions for a Candidate of the Ministry*, published in 1726,[2] has added interest as its author's last important work.

Many of his marked enthusiasms and antipathies are evident as his topics range from health rules to philosophical systems, from practical ways to succeed in the world to an impassioned plea for a united Christian church. The ripened thought of a man who has reas and written all his life, this last essay serves as the epitome of a lifetime of pulpit service, of interest in the world of books, and of ideological development. Here, in this last major attempt to be of service to God and man, are to be seen the author's lifelong loyalties to old authorities and the church of his fathers; on the other hand, here too, both in what Mather accepts and what he protests against, are the many evidences of the effect of changing times on religious and phillosophical thought. Both the practicality and the tolerance of the later eighteenth century are well foreshadowed.

This idea of helping young ministers-to-be and even recently ordained ministers by some sort of manual certainly was not original. In fact, the author excuses himself for outlining the studies that his

131

son Samuel (the ostensible beneriter of all this instruction) or any other candidate for a New England pulpit should undertake by noting that the best authority, Chytraeus,[3] was 120 years old. When the great question of ministerial duties finally is reached, Mather notes the "troop" of writers that have been before him, starting with Gregory and his famous *Pastoral Care*.[4] Consequently he feels the literature on the subject, although occasionally of value, to be too extensive for a young student to struggle through. He can, instead, turn to the *Manuductio*.

Nevertheless, like a number of Mather's more ambitious publications, this one does not immediately entice its readers. The long Latin preface of nineteen pages[5] dwells on its author's chiliastic beliefs: the approaching Second Coming of Christ and the Day of Judgment. Typical, too, of the mature Cotton Mather is his respectful admiration of German conservative pietism as shown by his enthusiastic tribute to Franckius and Halle University. Contemplation of this supposedly ideal place of learning led Mather to a major premise: good men must love and court all kinds of wisdom, with the love of God as the illumination of the mind. Then, dropping from this lofty level, he speaks against what he considers to be two modern corruptions of philosophy: systems of ethics that do not base goodness on religious tenets; and, equally annoying and dangerous, that mad freakishness that insists on metaphorical interpretation of the Bible.

The book proper starts with an impassioned plea for men to remember that the end of life is to glorify God, for without this controlling directive they will be beasts, almost completely brutish: "A little more Hair, and crawling upon all Four - and, what the Difference!" (5). If man is not to lower himself in this way, he must do every act of his life, eating, drinking, sleeping, reading, writing, visiting, as acts of service to his Lord; he must value his children and friends as part of Christ's Kingdom. Finally, after pages of impassioned pleading, Mather has his reader ask, "*What Good may I be capable of doing in the World?*" (21).

As in the *Essays to do Good*, the answer is for each man to start improving his own goodness and knowledge, then help his relatives, then members of any society to which he belongs, then his neighbors. The explanation of the "*Rational Mystery of Godliness*" is simple: God must be glorified, venerated, as generations of earlier Puritans had taught; but the humanitarian implications carried with this veneration are of the eighteenth century: "Whatever contributes unto the *Welfare* of *Mankind*, and such a *Relief* of their Miseries, as may give the Children of Men better *Opportunities* to Glorify Him, *This* also is to *Glorify* Him" (8).

Having given all this general advice, Mather turns his attention to his subject proper, the problems that face the young candidate in his preparation for the ministry. Before actually starting to outline the studies to be followed, the old minister has two warnings to give a serious student. First, whatever the young man learns in any field of knowledge he must keep in mind that he is doing so only for the service of God; each book he picks up, the same aim should be with him. In the seventeenth century this much-argued belief in the purpose of learning was the Puritan scholar's justification for spending so much of his time in study rather than in prayer or pastoral care of the congregation: whatever he learned would help him to understand the Bible and man, God's voice and his creation. Now in the eighteenth century Mather feels the need of a special warning to a more worldly age. Man should want the "illuminations" of knowledge not just "to gain a comfortable Subsistance in the World" or to be the recipient of other men's praise; he should want to become a better servant of God and "an instrument of Good unto others" (24 - 26).

The second warning is on a still more mundane level. Even if the student has "thus fixed the Right End" of his scholarly pursuits, he may still suffer a "Vile Impediment" in the entanglement of any "*Foolish Amour*." Marriage at this time may result in a very great calamity instead of the "very great *Felicity*" of a wiser choice (27).

I   "*Preparation for the Sanctuary*"

Thus dedicated to his studies, the celibate minister-to-be had much to learn. Languages, only the tools, came first. Latin and a good Latin style were essential, nor was there any doubt about an adequate knowledge of Greek. Earlier generations of New Englanders also had regarded Hebrew as a vital part of a minister's equipment for exegesis, but this tradition was declining. Mather bitterly notes that "a learned Man [is] almost afraid of owning that he has any thing of it, lest it should bring him under the Suspicion of being an Odd, Starv'd Lank sort of thing, who had lived only on *Hebrew Roots* all his Days" (30). But Mather, aptly citing what

Hebrew had meant to Luther, still protests that Hebrew and Syriac (Aramaic) are necessary for a full and accurate understanding of the Bible.

Modern languages are a completely different question. Mather advocates that one should learn them as need arises. Undoubtedly he was thinking of his own rapid acquiring of French and Spanish when he felt the time had come to attempt to proselytize foreign nations and their colonies. He does note, however, one cultural advantage in learning French: "There is no Man who has the *French Tongue*, but ordinarily he speaks the neater *English* for it" (32).

Sensibly enough, before starting to discuss the fields of knowledge in which the intelligent preacher should be proficient and the minimum number of books to be read upon each subject, Mather suggests that the young man "find out a *North-West Passage*" to help himself. He recommends Alsted's[6] encyclopedic volumes as being a compendium of true learning.

Mather's theories of what was important in education, what unimportant, led him to suggest other obvious ways to conserve time. Certain sciences (using the word in the general sense of branches of knowledge) could be skimmed over quickly. With his usual outspoken courage of his convictions, he does not hesitate either to run counter to Harvard's time-honored curriculum or to oppose popular educational theories of the 1720s as he selects which fields should not be allowed to consume too many hours.

The first subject to be dismissed briefly is rhetoric (34 - 35). Unlike earlier emphasis on simplicity in pulpit oratory, elaborate rhetoric was becoming fashionable. According to Mather, instead if reading many books on rhetorical theory, the young minister-to-be should naturally turn to the Bible, for in Scripture can be found both the sublime and the more truly moving figures of speech, taken from life. Only to be fashionably aware of the contemporary nomenclature of these tropes is there any call to read books of instruction.

In protesting (35 - 36) against devoting too much time to logic, the second subject to be passed over briefly, Mather is attacking long-entrenched Harvard educational practices. From the foundation of the college no secular study had been held in greater respect.[7] But the young man following the precepts of the *Manuductio* can almost ignore logic, for it consists, claims the author, of merely proving what one already knows; at best, it may provide material for arguing, and even then the truth often is distorted. Consequently, if the young man reads a few authorities on logic,[8] his wits will be sharpened sufficiently.

Metaphysics (37), by some considered the queen of sciences, as Mather candidly admits, is another subject with which young men should not linger. In order to avoid confusion, the student should confine himself to a very few writers[9]—unless he really wants "to weave . . . more Cobwebs" into his brain.

The dangers of dwelling upon rhetoric, logic, and metaphysics lay in wasting time (always a sin in Mather's mind) and in becoming confused. Even worse were the perils of dwelling on ethics (37 - 38), with its pretense of offering a faith without Christ; here the Puritan instructor is echoing a very highly respected Puritan authority, William Ames,[10] whose voluminous works are frequently recommended throughout the *Manuductio*. In obvious criticism of the teaching of ethics as a separate study at Harvard, Mather counsels his young man at most to glance at the standard college texts (which included the works of the renowned More[11]). Instead of wasting time on such books, the wise student should turn to the Bible and to the German Pietist Arndt,[12] presumably to learn to love his fellow man. Proper behavior, after all, is "all *Embryo'd* in that one Word, MODESTY: which Renders every one his *due*, and assumes nothing *undue* to ones self." In fact, "the most exact and constant *Rules of Behaviour*, will be found *Rules of Christianity*. . . . Every *Christian* as far as he keeps his own *Rules* will be so far a *Gentleman*" (38).

Having thus summarily disposed of the study of ethics by simplifying it to the Golden Rule and to good manners, much as his admired Newton advocated, Mather turned to the more complex subject of the place of poetry in a young man's education (38 - 44). It must be remembered that Mather all his life was fond of writing verse, that he knew Horace and Vida on the art of poetry, and that he had read the poets he condemns. On the other hand, he could recommend neither the teaching of the pagans nor the worldliness of many Restoration writers. Therefore he treads a middle path by advising the true scholar "to make a little *Recreation* of *Poetry*" in the midst of more "painful" studies. He can always sharpen his senses and polish his style by constructing an occasional epigram.

But a young man should be careful that he does not develop a "*Boundless* and *Sickly* Appetite" for the "Passionate and *Measured* Pages." Some of the Muses with whom he might associate "are no better than *Harlots*." Homer's morals are deplorable; Virgil has led

many astray. Nevertheless, beauty and much antiquarian lore are to
be found in their works. Ovid, however, is worse than these epic
poets. His epistles have a tendency to excite and foment "Impure
Flames" in one's bosom. Also in the library of the Prince of
Darkness are most modern plays as well as all the "*Romances* and
Novels and *Fictions*" of the day; but even more evil are coarse and
"unclean" but popular satires,[13] which should not be allowed to
crawl, like Egyptian toads, into a good man's chamber. (He does
not mention that this despised doggerel often mocked Puritans of
various sects, especially by accusing them of hypocrisy.) Of all the
poets, he has words of unqualified praise only for his contemporary
and correspondent, Sir Richard Blackmore.[14] (Milton, whom he had
read,[15] is completely ignored as a poet.)

By way of a parenthesis Mather then offers his theories on style
(44 - 47). As in the *Magnalia*, he feels it necessary to justify his own
manner of writing:

The Writer pretends not unto *Reading*, yet he could not have writ as he
does if had not *Read* very much in his Time; and his Composures are not
only a *Cloth of Gold*, but also stuck with as many *Jewels*, as the Gown of a
Russian Embassador. (44)

He has only scorn for fashionable books of "Superfluous *Margin*"
that offer none of his "*Massy Way of Writing*." Then, more objec-
tively, he notes that ideally "Every Man will have his own *Style*,
which will distinguish him as much as his Gate *[sic]*, and this way of
writing should prove satisfactory if there is an "Easy Conveyance"
of his ideas. For example, take Seneca and Cicero - each pleases in
his own way. Finally, critics are not to be taken too seriously: not
only do they disagree among themselves but even those of some
scholarship can be outrageously mistaken in their fault-finding.

In his next field of study, "natural philosophy" (47 - 52), a term
he defined very broadly, Mather has at last reached a subject to
which he can wholeheartedly encourage devotion. He has reservations, however. With some violence he denounces Aristotelian
philosophy as having been faultily preserved and so in many points
"*Unintelligible*, and forever in almost all things *Unprofitable*" (49).
The wise student will get as "thorough an Insight" as possible into
"the *Principles* of our *Perpetual Dictator*, the Incomparable Sr.
Isaac Newton."[16] Then, too, the worthy ideas of such modern
religiously minded philosophers as Robert Boyle[17] and John Ray[18]

can be found in the transactions of the Royal Society. As a summation, and with the author showing no undue modesty, "the largest Collection, I have yet seen of the *Discoveries* which the last Age has made in Philosophy" has been gathered in Mather's own *The Christian Philosopher* (1721). In other words, the older Peripatetic dicta that had dominated philosophy and physics until the seventeenth century should be contemned and the new experimental philosophy studied as completely as possible as it developed.

Having dwelt upon philosophy, Mather does little with mathematics (52 - 53), although this elderly Puritan guider of young men recommends the study of mathematics not only as a strengthener of men's minds but also as an improver of their morals. "It seems that . . . Intense *Applications* and *Speculations* are inconsistent with Debaucheries."

Briefly treated, too, is the subject of astronomy (53 - 54), although Mather feels that it is necessary for men "to soar upwards." On the other hand, astrology (54 - 55) is to be condemned as "all Futility, All Impiety." Even blazing stars or comets are not portentous, although they may be used in preaching as presages or warnings of evil to come.

Of all the branches of knowledge, geography (55 - 57) seemed to Mather the easiest to learn, and yet to be of some importance. A background for scriptural studies would be of value to all ministers, and so their faithful instructor offers a number of authorities on the Holy Land, including one of some lasting fame, Thomas Fuller,[19] author of *Pisgah Sight*. When information is wanted about the modern world of England and her colonies, Mather suggests that Camden[20] is "good Entertainment," but he is harshly critical of a popular contemporary historian, Oldmixon,[21] who, alas, had once spoken scornfully of Mather's *Magnalia*. Despite the ease with which geography could be conquered, and the possibility of reading false accounts, there were two quite different advantages to the study: knowledge of other countries would certainly improve a man's conversation and might arouse in him missionary zeal.

At least Mather had come to definite conclusions on the value of most branches of knowledge, but he was uncertain about music: "For MUSIC, I know not what well to say. —Do as you please" (57). Although he does include it among the studies of the young pastor-to-be, he apparently is not thinking in terms of theory or of history; the studying was to result in performance. The man who would not waste God's time admits that there may be

"Refreshment" in playing an instrument, and so God may be better served thereafter. Vocal music is quite another matter. Church singing on the Sabbath is not enough. "For I would not have a Day pass you without *Singing*, but so as at the same time to *make a Melody in your Heart unto the Lord.* . . ."

As a climax to the secular studies of a minister, Mather stresses history (58 - 71), "one of the most Needful and Useful Accomplishments, for a Man that would serve GOD as you Propose to do." The tyro should begin with concise universal histories;[22] then he can proceed to "Volumes of larger Dimensions."[23] As the next step, there are the histories of particular countries, and Mather offers what he considers to be the authorities for France, Spain, Holland, the Ottoman Empire, Abyssinia, Russia, China, America, Scotland, Ireland, and England—in that order. The Puritan world was not as small and self-centered as is sometimes imagined: Mather even notes that there are "several small *Story-tellers*" for Persia and Hindustan.

Everything that the young student reads should not, of course, be accepted without due consideration. In evaluating histories of foreign nations, the intelligent student will remember that Jesuit writers may not be presenting their facts without prejudice; in reading English history, bias against Puritans and Puritanism should be taken into account. Proud as he was of any demonstration of his own scholarship, Mather takes pleasure in pointing out a number of errors and contradictions in classical and modern histories. He is bitter about Josephus, the first-century Jewish historian, but his real scorn is for the anti-Puritan Anthony à Wood,[24] whose outpourings cannot be sufficiently despised and abhored (64).

All this reading of "civil history" is but preparation for becoming "well-acquainted" with church history (65 - 69). Some men may be satirical about the "many large volumes" that seem only to record the squabbles of the clergy, but Mather wants it clearly known that he is not of their mind. In his eyes ignorance of church history was a "Blemish" that came near to disqualifying a man from the pulpit. Again the kindly mentor offers general compendiums as overall guides, and then suggests the specialists, from Eusebius, the fourth-century "Father of Church History," down to the contemporary Gilbert Burnet.[25] To be included, too, are the martyrologies.

But Mather has not finished the categories of history that should be studied. From the lives of martyrs the natural course is to continue reading biographies. If Samuel Clarke's[26] collection of lives is more "Dull & Lifeless" than most books, other biographies of greater worth had been written in the preceding century, including Thomas Fuller's *The Worthies of England* (1662) and Izaak Walton's *Lives* (1640 - 1678); nor should a still later book, *Parentator*, the life of Increase Mather published by the writer in 1724, be neglected.

Then, with some extra collections of histories to dip into casually, and some chronologies and lexicons in his library to aid his accuracy, the would-be minister can feel that in this one respect, his knowledge of the past, he is ready for his pastoral duties.

Before leading the youthful student into the *"Fair Havens* of *Theology,"* Mather has two practical suggestions (71 - 75). First, as the young man reads he should copy noteworthy passages into a bound book; in other words, he should keep a Quotidiana or commonplace book (as all Harvard students were encouraged to do). With the practicality of experience, he suggests entering one numbered quotation after another and then indexing by topic, rather than arranging headings and afterwards trying to fit entries under them, the more usual way. Second, as he had urged in his *Bonifacius (Essays to do Good)* with greater detail, it was wise for an earnest man to form a "sodality." By this Mather again means to do as he had done as a young man (and his father before him): gather six or seven "Sober, Ingenious, and Industrious Young Men" into a club to discuss some question in any proposed field, from philology to biblical curiosities. (In the *Bonifacius* the suggested purpose of such clubs or societies had been moral; here their educational value is pointed out as members would learn from each other, become certain of their own information, and gain skill as speakers.)

Having with these two practical asides interrupted the program of studies, Mather quickly returns to his promised discussion of theology (75 - 89). The student naturally will start with the Bible, but no cursory reading is satisfactory. Each verse, each clause, should be considered separately for its lessons of piety, and these in turn should be turned into prayers. And the hopeful man of God can do yet more. He can try to discover in each line the emotions of piety that the Holy Spirit aroused in the man who wrote it, and there can be an attempt to duplicate this emotion, this piety. Not that this soul exercise, truly valuable as it may be, is enough without scholarship for guidance. There are biblical commentaries to be studied, comprehensive ones by Henry and Poole,[27] then specialized ones devoted to specific books.

Before a man can qualify as an educated minister, much more is
to be read. Many are the helpful writers in systematic theology.
Polemic divinity is a large field, too, ranging from books that give a
"general insight" into the problem, such as Mather's own *Supplies
from the Tower of David* (1708, 1721), to the arguments useful in
combating particular schisms and controversies. Still another extensive field of reading lies in patristic literature. The church fathers
are to be studied, despite their manifest errors, especially
Theodoret[28] for his exposition of the Bible, Chrysostom[29] (the great
preacher), and Augustine[30] (with emphasis on the *Confessions,
Meditations,* and *De Civitate Dei*).

II *Wisdom for a Young Minister*

After all these years of study, this *"preparation for the Sanctuary,"* the young scholar must not waste his hard-earned
knowledge (89 - 93). Nothing is more important than that his sermons be well studied—and well prayed about. He may preach in
turn upon every line in the Bible, or he may choose particular parts
of Scripture that are extremely "rich," having an "admirable variety of important *Subjects.*" In either case, he should not linger for
some weeks upon a text, for such "tedious Amplification, must need
leave much of the *sacred Field* unplough'd upon" (93). And in
planning the year's sermons he should leave some Sabbaths or
Lecture-Days free for especially timely occasional subjects.

Whatever the minister preaches upon, he should include much of
Christ (93 - 96). "Yea, let the Motto of your whole Ministry, be,
CHRIST IS ALL." This fervid Christology, this urging that the
Savior be the all-important sermon topic, reflects Mather's sincere,
basic belief, but it can also be seen as a Boston Congregationalist's
struggle against the rising deism of the eighteenth century. Cotton
Mather was living during a period in which many educated men,
interested in the new science, rarely went so far as to deny God the
Creator, but they might, often more or less tacitly, question belief
in the Trinity.

Then, as a corollary to this emphasis to be put upon Christ,
Mather urges the young minister to devote much of his preaching to
the doctrine of Grace (96 - 102). In other words, no part of piety
should be more important than the traditional Calvinist doctrine
that man is not saved by his works but by his having been chosen to
be in a state of grace or, in other words, of the Elect; he must,

however, prepare and be ready to accept this covenant made with God through Christ's intercession. Mather complains of such modern books as tend to dress up "our Doctrine of *Predestination* in Fallacious and Invidious Terms." Such books should be avoided. And then he proceeds to offer some twenty-six treatises by English writers of the previous century, all on practical divinity and all orthodoxly Calvinist in tenets. To these any preacher might find it to his advantage to add over a dozen volumes by contemporary Scottish theologians, also safely in the same Calvinist tradition.

Having thus removed the young generation from any temptation to be adversely critical of the basic Calvinist doctrine of predestination, Mather returned to other bits of advice that should be heeded by any tyro aiming for success in the pulpit (102 - 105). In order to be certain to use sufficient scriptural references to prove or illustrate points, he should make use of various helpful concordances. So that he can make his points "sensible to the lowest and meanest Capacities, yea, to all *Flesh*," he must use similitudes or comparisons. And he must remember to appeal to everyone's emotions, to "spread the *Nets of Salvation*" so movingly that the congregation "must have their *Hearts burn within* them, & they must be *Hearts of Stone* indeed, if they take not Fire immediately" (104).

Mather has more advice of a very practical nature (105 - 106). Sermons should be well delivered, with dignity, with correct pronunciations. "Let your *Notes* be little other than a *Quiver*, on which you may cast your Eye now and then, to see what *Arrow* is to be next fetch'd from thence: and then with your Eye as much as may be on them whom you speak to, Let it be shot away, with a *Vivacity* becoming *One in Earnest*" (106). Finally, the peroration of each sermon must appeal forcefully to the conscience of listeners, for each hearer has a "flaming Preacher" in his bosom that will help "wondrously" the preacher in the pulpit.

Preaching is not the only duty of a minister, as Mather well knew, but it was by far the most important one in Puritan minds. He discusses only very briefly pastoral visiting and catechizing (106 - 108); then he has more to say about praying (108 - 13). Whole days should be set apart from "Interviews with Heaven." If a man has days of supplication, he must not forget days of thanksgiving. In fact, there is only one great danger in prayer, that men may fall into dependence on the "*Lifeless Forms of any Liturgy*."

Having read much, preached well, prayed long and earnestly, the poor minister faces one more difficulty in an ungrateful, underpaying congregation (113 - 15). But he must not "ruin the Success of the Gospel" by resorting to the law for his promised pay even if he feels that he is in danger of starvation. For God will provide. (Although Mather often suspected the laity, especially his own congregation, of being "Monsters of Ingratitude," here he is being candid rather than unduly pessimistic. True, in his own time of severest financial need, his church had generously rescued him. Nevertheless, cases of controversy over pay between congregations and ministers were fairly common; very occasionally legal steps were taken to secure promised support. Many more pastors in poor churches must have accepted their poverty. At one time, about 1712,[13] Mather had a private list of seven ministers in decided need. Having been given some money to disburse charitably, he chose by lot four of the seven to receive this temporary easing of their situations.)

III   The Cardinal Necessity: An Ecumenical Spirit

After his homely display of the very human side of congregations and ministers and especially of himself and his feeling about pastoral relationships, Mather suddenly soars (115 - 19) into a remarkable attack on the "Antichristian Spirit of Sectarism." He had often made his pleas for tolerance,[32] but never as forcefully. He seems to have grown with his own teaching as he urges the young minister to preach so that he will bring all men together in *"Peace on Earth from a Good Will in Men towards one another."* It is now the *"First born"* of his wishes that the *"Everlasting Gospel"* be so presented to the godly that they "tho' of *different Perswasions* in *lesser Points, . . .* embrace one another upon the *Generous Maxims* of it, and keep *lesser Points* in a due *Subordination* unto the *Superiour Maxims"* (116).

This union "among all Parties of true CHRISTIANS, however they may be Denominated or Distinguished," is not to come as a result of "that loathsome thing, A *Lifeless Religion.*" The new *"Brotherly Fellowship* with all Good Men"* is to be a matter of positive piety, and it will carry with it the necessary corollary of civil liberty:

I Declare for the just Liberties of *Mankind,* and of our Nations: And for a Christian Encouragement in the *Church* for all that observe the Grand MAXIMS of PIETY, accompanied with a free *Indulgence* of *Civil Rights* in the *State,* unto all that approve themselves Faithful *Subjects* and Honest

Neighbours, and such Inoffensive Livers, that *Humane Society* cannot complain of Disturbance from them (119).

Then, with great optimism, Mather proposes a definite union of certain churches. He suggests that Calvinists and Lutherans can be reconciled, for their differences, he claims, rise from what they emphasize in doctrine, rather than from true differences in belief. In a short debate "Master Lutheran" and "Master Calvinist" set forth their tenets—and find themselves in surprising agreement (121 - 24).

Having devoted several pages to the question of Calvinist-Lutheran accord, Mather came back to his entreaty for true piety: "Let your *Feet stand in a large Place,* and, *Add unto your Faith, Godliness, and unto Godliness, Brotherly-kindness, and unto your Brotherly-kindness, Charity"* (125 - 26).

With this "true piety" and interdenominational viewpoint, the ideal church will really enjoy Christian fellowship:

And let the *Table* of the Lord have no *Rails* about it, that shall hinder a Godly *Independent,* and *Presbyterian,* and *Episcopalian,* and *Antipedobaptist,* and *Lutheran,* from sitting down together there (127).

Furthermore, he believed that he was not alone in this vision of Christian fellowship, that there were "Hundreds of Thousands of Generous Minds" ready for this ecumenical concept, with only the "Mean, Little, Narrow Souls, that know no *Religion"* wishing to maintain their sectarianism (129).

It is not surprising after his powerful appeal for unity among men of faith that Mather, ever the student, backed his plea by urging the reading of similar ideas (129 - 30). Specifically, he recommends (in addition to a number of commentators on the Bible) Thomas Aquinas,[33] who as early as the thirteenth century tried to reconcile faith and reason; the mystic Thomas à Kempis,[34] to whom the Pietists felt they owed much; and finally, the German and Dutch "orthodox" (conservative) pietists, including Gerhardt, Spener, and Voetius.[35]

IV *Very Practical Advice for an Aspiring Young Man*

Abruptly Cotton Mather leaves all mystic philosophers and European pietists with their hopes for one Christian world. The *Manuductio* ends on some very sensible notes; in fact. the type of practical wisdom displayed emphasizes how much men of the eighteenth century such as Mather and Pope and Franklin had in common as they faced a competitive world.

First, Mather makes good use of his then unpublished *Angel of Bethesda* by offering what is practically a synopsis (130 - 36) of the rules of health in that lengthy volume: live abstemiously; exercise, especially by moderate riding, for "the *Saddle* is the *Seat* of *Health*"; have family purges, as Bacon had advocated; use much cold water internally and externally; eat vegetables and grains, little salt meat; drink milk, for a "*Milk-Diet* is for the most part some of the wholesomest in the world!" Do not smoke, and he cites various authorities on the evils coming from that "slovenly practice": "The *Memory* is impaired, the *Stomach* violated, the *Brain* exiccated, and the *Life* shortened; and the *Offspring* Damnified" (134). The taking of snuff is almost as harmful, injuring the nerves especially; on every snuffbox, that "Pandora's Box," the motto might appear "A LEADER TO THE COFFIN."

More general advice follows. Above all, do not eat too much! Remember that tranquility and serenity of mind have much to do with good health. And if one does fall sick, it is intelligent to take care of oneself quickly and to take time to recuperate fully.

Not only should the sagacious minister try to preserve his health but he should also be prudent in general (136 - 42). This helpful virtue may best be learned from the Book of Proverbs in the Bible and from Bacon's *Essays*, but if this pair of instructors does not satisfy, other literatures will supply helpful maxims. The man who would succeed in this world must be good-natured; he must do nothing rashly or in a passion; he would be foolish to waste time in contentions and quarrels and squabbles. Anyway, the astute man does not betray that he knows who has spoken against him or injured him. If he does, his enemy will only hate him the more, trying to justify the first injury, and so reconciliation becomes impossible. Instead of seeking revenge, a good man (a Cotton Mather, by implication) will prove his learning and serviceableness by the books he produces.

If prudence is a somewhat negative virtue that calls for many a "do not," Mather in his mature sagacity and as an experienced minister also has a stock of positive advice to offer any rising young man (142 - 46). It behooves the latter to be sociable, especially with his superiors; to have a supply of questions on hand to submit humbly in order to guide conversations advantageously; and not to be too positive in making his points. (Mather and Franklin[36] certainly were in accord here, but Franklin seems to have carried out the precept more successfully.) He should have a bosom friend, a wise and good person, but put a stop to his confidences before he falls into any man's power. The young minister should speak well of everyone, but not be "too Copious" or "too Early" in his commendations. He needs to take care to keep to his ministry, for if a clergyman becomes a slave to any "Man of Quality," the latter will abandon him when he ceases to be a convenient tool.

As one more practical point, in order to accomplish his good ends any minister must have "an Inexhaustible Store of *Stories*, accommodated unto all the Purposes of the *Profitable* and the *Agreeable*, and have the Skill of *telling* them *Handsomely*, and with a *Deliberate, Expressive, Unstumbling Brevity*." In this way not only will he ingratiate himself at every appearance, but he will also obtain "almost any *Request*" that has such a witty introduction.

Finally, and at no moment in all his writing is Mather more pleasantly human as he accepts his own limitations, it is a point of true wisdom to admit that a thinking, prayerful man will have to learn to live with "Two *Heaps*, An *Heap* of UNINTELLIGIBLES; and an *Heap* of INCURABLES." On the first heap must be thrown the "*Unaccountable* and *Incomprehensible* Things" that people do; on the second, "*Unperswadeable* People" who remain obstinate in the face of all counsel and reason. "Leave them there. And so do you go on to *do as well as you can*, what you have to do. Let not the *Crooked Things* that can't be made straight, encumber you" (146 - 147). (Was he thinking of his failure to save his beloved son Increase from the worst kinds of folly? Of his passionate third wife with her fits of frenzy, alternately loving and hating him? Or just of parishioners and fellow ministers and men in power who so often looked upon life with different eyes from his?)

With the only deliberate smile in the whole book of general counsel and positive recommendations, Cotton Mather ends:

'Tis a Trespass on the *Rules of Prudence*, never to know, *when to have done*. Wherefore, *I have done!*

V   *Critical Reaction to the Manuductio*

And what he had finished is more than a manual for ministers, although his avowed purpose has kept many readers from the little volume. Earlier critics, too, perhaps wary of a brief "manual" that endeavors to cover so much ground, were inclined to limit their evaluations to praise of Mather's vigorous style and clarity. Moses Coit Tyler,[37] who as a whole felt extremely alien to Cotton Mather but who was always sensitive to style, praised the *Manuductio* as "written heartily," with real enthusiasm, so that it became "the most vigorous and entertaining book that he [Mather] ever wrote." Tyler, however, does not really discuss the book, but contents himself with citing some amusingly forceful passages on the corruptions Aristotelian philosophy had suffered and on the falsehoods that various historians had presented as truth. Barrett Wendell, Mather's most sympathetic critic, ignores the book completely. Kenneth Murdock[38] cites Tyler's favorable judgment and then dismisses the book with brief praise as "an exercise in unvarnished prose" that presents an "eminently sane understanding of the ideal of scholarship."

More recent critics, including Perry Miller[39] (whose interpretation and evaluation of seventeenth- and eighteenth-century American literature have been influential in forming later judgments), are recognizing how indicative the book is of Mather's mature development not only in tolerance and religious philosophy but also in the plain practicality so typical of the eighteenth century.

As is true of his *Bonifacius (Essays to do Good)* and his *Christian Philosopher*, the *Manuductio* is remarkably terse, accomplishing much in its 149 pages. It is far more than a reading prospectus for ministers-to-be and has far more significance than its author ever suspected. In this last treatise Cotton Mather has managed to show, with amazing transparency, the opposite sides of his own mind and character, and these contrasts, although seldom found so obviously in one man, are at least to a degree typical of his time.

Mather's ideal young man, fashioned so closely on his author, may have to do an amazing amount of reading about the past, especially in history and theology, but he also has to keep up with current developments in natural philosophy, the explanations of the universe that the best scientific minds of his own age were offering and trying to reconcile with the Bible. Furthermore, that young man cannot become a bookwork; he should develop the practical wisdom to control himself and, as much as possible, the society in which he lives. Without loss of integrity, he can (or so Mather tells him) ingratiate himself with the right people, become successful in the popular, mundane sense of the word. In short, he should be capable of being both scholar and man of the world.

He apparently is under the necessity of believing absolutely in predestination, although his Calvinism need not stress damnation for the nonelect and may permit him to believe that the desire for salvation is practically synonymous with the achievement. He must hold firmly to the tenet that he is saved by Grace alone, not by works; but he must devote his life to good works for his fellow men. And he ought to be able to combine his fervid belief in the correctness of his own church with the broadest tolerance for all other Protestant churches. Consequently, his moral and ethical obligation is to combine Calvinism and conservative pietism, with its emphasis on tolerance and service to man; and by so doing he will reach the apotheosis of Christianity.

If Cotton Mather saw any contradictions in his proposals for the ideal man of God, any difficulties in his path, he gives no sign of his awareness. He seems very certain that no right-thinking individual could or would disagree with him.

CHAPTER 12

Cotton Mather: "Publick Friend" and "Inexhaustible Source of Divine Flame & Vigour"

CRITICISM of Cotton Mather as an individual, as a leader in his community, as a man of letters, and as a scientist has been indeed varied. (As a minister and church leader his ability was not denied in colonial times, nor has it been questioned by later Congregationalists.) In his own day and for the rest of the eighteenth century and into the nineteenth century, despite some dissident voices, he was accepted as one of the last great Puritans. But during the nineteenth century, with the rise of Romanticism and Transcendentalism (and the distrust of formal religion), American critics for the most part were decidedly anti-Puritan and so out of sympathy with the Mather dynasty. These limited evaluations of Cotton Mather were largely based on his *Diary*, his witchcraft writings, *Bonifacius*, (Essays to do Good), and the *Magnalia*. In the twentieth century attempts at a fairer judgment began as scholarship tried to consider his varied contributions to science and the relation of science to religion, to biography, to history, to social benevolence; in modern criticism, while the *Magnalia*, still regarded as his most outstanding work, has been lauded both as history and as epic, *The Christian Philosopher*, the *Manuductio*, his letters to the Royal Society (including his advocacy of inoculation as a preventive for smallpox), and his many lesser publications have helped to form appraisals of this complex man of many accomplishments.

Unfortunately, in a number of ways Cotton Mather hurt his own reputation by his frankness in his yearly diaries. He recorded all his moments of weakness, his possible sins, with vehement regret—and with sufficient ambiguity to arouse a question of just how severe the
148

fall from virtue had been; he also listed, with annoying complacency if not self-applause, all his good intentions, from carrying sweets for children he might meet on his pastoral calls to seeing that the Long Island pulpits were adequately filled. As the years went on, he also cried out again and again that he was abused and humiliated, almost beyond human endurance, with the comparison with Christ naturally coming to his mind.

The most dramatic and the lengthiest of these jeremiads was compiled in 1724, when his neurotic third wife was making life especially difficult for him, when he was so badly in debt that he was in danger of losing his prized library, when he had just endured an "Hour of Darkness" as his very faith faltered. He carefully listed all his sufferings, greater, he was sure, than any other man's. The tale of woe is amazingly full: his poverty and threatened loss of his library, of course; he is abused by the "female sex" and by his relatives; he has no comfort in his children; he has received manifold expressions of aversion from everyone, including his Scottish friends; both the government and Harvard scorn him; his company is little sought; no helping hands aid him, but books are written against him; and he is certain that everyone is pointing him out as the most afflicted man on earth.

Cotton Mather, unlike most men, recorded in full this passing mood of black despair, and the very wording of his sorrows seemingly comforted him as he felt his closeness to Christ as another Man of Sorrows. His complaints surely should not be read as indicative of his failure or his lack of popularity in his own day. As a matter of record, loyal members of his congregation paid his debts, and by this "helping hand" saved his library; if he was passed over several times in the selection of a new president for Harvard, he was offered the presidency of Yale (and some would regard this as an honor not to be scorned); reports of the comfort and solace that his little instructional and devotional books were to many of his parishioners, young and old, came his way as well as acknowledgment from many that they had been saved through his preaching. Far from abandoned by his surviving family and friends, in his last illness he had the devotion of his only living son, Samuel, his nephew Mather Byles, and a number of young local ministers.

It is true that Cotton Mather met criticism during his lifetime: for example, for the frequency of his publication, for his credulity in believing some of the tales of the "possessed" victims of witchcraft, for his advocacy of inoculation. In sharp contrast to the revered standing of earlier colonial ministers (during the first fervor of New England Puritanism), an eighteenth-century minister no longer was the most respected man in town, above mockery and lampooning. This change was not Cotton Mather's personal failure; society itself had changed and was still changing economically and socially. Nevertheless, when Cotton Mather died in 1728, effusive tributes were paid to the "principal ornament" and the greatest scholar of the colonies, "the first minister in the town, first in age, in gifts, in grace." He was extolled for his "exalted piety" and his "flaming sermons." His extensive charity, catholic to all good men, and his "singular goodness" of temper were recalled. His "grave or smiling countenance," his "gracious and reviving looks," would be much missed.

The tide of really adverse criticism did not begin until a century after his death. Over the years the range of charges against him has been extraordinarily diverse. He has been charged with being a prejudiced Calvinist, narrow-minded and eagerly damning all non-Calvinists to hell. Of course he was a Calvinist and so believed his Bible that there was a hell as well as a heaven. He also said that every man had the right to his own beliefs, unhampered by civil authority. By the end of his life he was such a "mild" Calvinist, asking men to use their reason and preaching that men were saved by faith but the desire to be saved was an indication of their salvation, praising nature as the great manifestation of God, that he has been called the first American deist, an equally horrendous accusation in many minds.

He has been labeled a hypocrite by men incapable of recognizing religious ecstacy or the absolute belief in the power of prayer. On the other hand, he has been charged with breaking down religion and substituting a morality of benevolence. He would be surprised at this last calumny, for he certainly did not mean to do other than to further true religious faith: if, as he said, the City of God admitted only those with good deeds to their credit, he was equally convinced that no man could get as far as the Gate without saving grace.

He has also been reproached with being unchristian (if not unstable) in his bursts of vituperative anger at all whom he classified as enemies. In the seventeenth and eighteenth centuries harsh name-calling characterized most disputes. In addition, Cotton Mather more often than not felt that he was defending the very existence of the Congregational churches, sometimes even the survival of the New England colonies. Then, too, he was frequently defending his father; psychologists explain that a response of fury to criticism of one's family is a form of self-defense, a protection of one's own self-esteem. Experience also teaches us that this fury may be in inverse degree to our own private (perhaps even unrecognized) opinion of the rightness or wrongness of the person under criticism. His *Diary* shows that by 1713 Cotton Mather (correctly or incorrectly) thought his father needed protective guidance, most respectfully managed. Two other points about Cotton's easily provoked temper deserve to be noted: he had at least resolved early in life not to waste time in quarrels; and he did pray for his "enemies."

He has been accused of being antidemocratic, of believing in a classed society, of acting as if education promoted intelligent leadership. (How many educated Englishmen in the eighteenth century would have disagreed with him?) Nevertheless, he argued all his life for more local schools and for better-attended schools; he not only preached and wrote that Negroes, free or slave, should have a basic education but he also established a night school for them.

He has been belittled as an amateur, ridiculous scientist, accepting any tall tale that came his way, including reports of two-headed snakes.[1] Cotton Mather recognized fully his limitations as a busy clergyman, far away in America from the center of scientific inquiry. Despite these obvious handicaps, through his reading he was able to appreciate the most advanced scientific ideas of his day, always respecting Baconian thought and methods, thinking of Newton as mankind's "perpetual dictator." He even managed to achieve four scientific "firsts"—or at least "firsts" in the colonies: he recognized the existence of animalculae or germs (as the conveyors of disease), advocated the use of inoculation against smallpox, observed the hybridization and cross-pollination of plants, and reported on the nesting habits of pigeons.

Many critics have smiled at the individuality of Cotton Mather's style of writing. He believed that every man should have his own gait in writing, but as a matter of fact he had a number of gaits, ranging from the ornate, baroque style of the *Magnalia*, to the less-decorated style of his later books (although by their purpose these are heavily weighted with citings and quotations), to the much simpler style of the sermons and instructional books. But whenever he preached, whatever he wrote, he had the great virtue of clarity:

his congregation in the Old North Church understood him, and readers more than 250 years later, agreeing with him or not, understand exactly what he is trying to convey. However much he wrote, he was always aware of the question of style; in fact, he wrote the first colonial essay on this topic. He also was the first New Englander to appreciate Milton's *Paradise Lost* to the point of quoting from and adapting passages from Milton's epic to benefit *his* epic, the *Magnalia*.

No one can deny the validity of critical accusations that Cotton Mather, a man who professed the deepest religious reverence, was guilty of the sin of pride. Of course he was conceited, descendant of the Cottons and Mathers, with his D.D. and his F.R.S., the possessor of the best library in New England, acknowledged by all, friends and rivals, to be the most erudite man in Massachusetts, preaching to a large, appreciative congregation, publishing at least once a month. He tried to be humble, face down in his study, pleading (usually in vain) with his Maker for the life of his beloved wife or for the recovery of one of his "little birds," most of whom stayed so briefly with him; or pleading more successfully for the survival of a manuscript or the publication of one of his books. But soon his own Angel was comforting him, giving him a "particular faith" to believe what he wanted to believe.

Undoubtedly Cotton Mather's most annoying trait of mind is closely connected with his pride—pride in what he could accomplish and pride in how good he could be. He preached moderation, but in setting his own goals he saw no reason to set any limitations. Especially, he could and would carry out every biblical precept fully, to what seemed to him its logical culmination.

If man should pray to his Maker, then the more frequent the praying the better—prayers in church; frequent gathering of the family together for prayers at home; extra prayer meetings at night, of course; days of private fasting and praying; after a while, night vigils of prayer. Then, too, one could train oneself to accompany every act of daily living with an appropriate prayer and to pray automatically for every passerby in the street, just as one could discipline oneself to fall asleep at night in meditation on the glory of the Savior.

If sermons are the Holy Spirit speaking through the preacher, a clarification of faith, a means to reform, then the more sermons the better, delivered and heard (and printed). Surely four or five sermons a week are better than one? (In this theory he was far from being alone in colonial Massachusetts.)

If it is a virtue, a service to God and man, to publish one book of purpose, what about the glorious virtue, the overwhelming service, of some 400 publications?

If it is right to keep the Covenant, to show one was of the Elect, by doing good deeds, then again the more good deeds the better. One way to accomplish these is to organize one's thoughts and energy. Organization always brings about results. Every day of the week should have its own category of virtuous acts. (As a result he has been called that most annoying of men, the professional do-gooder, with one bitter critic going so far as to say that poor Cotton had the soul of a Salvation Army colonel.)

If the Bible teaches "Love thy Neighbor," surely the Negroes living in your family are your closest neighbors? And if you love them, can you deny them the education that will make Christians of them? (Two hundred fifty years later black historians questioned how much harm Cotton Mather had done to the Negro cause by establishing this close relationship of the Christian church and the status of the Negro.)

If the Bible reveals that there will be a Second Coming of Christ, Who will reign on earth for a thousand years, surely preparation for this "Imcomparable Blessedness" is in order. And if the Bible, as interpreted by eminent Calvinist scholars, says that before this Millenium the Jews, once the elect of God, will be converted to Christianity and the power of the Beast of Rome destroyed, then surely all efforts should be made to convert Jews and Roman Catholics. The problems of language and effective distribution of proselytizing literature might make lesser men hesitate, but not Cotton Mather. (And his practical friend Samuel Sewall agreed with him to the point of financing the printing of the little pamphlets that were to accomplish so much.)

If the Bible has many references to angels, good angels, protective angels, guiding angels, surely Cotton Mather, always the Lord's devoted servant and mouthpiece, should not be surprised that God had supplied him with a special angel to help him interpret God's will. As he said, he saw the the doctrine of angels more clearly than some men.

If the Bible mentions witches (admittedly with a little question about the meaning of the word), if people confess to being witches, if one can actually see the work of the Devil, if theologians and more worldly scholars all agree that there are witches, what sane person would doubt their existence? The question of identifying these agents of the Devil raises great difficulty, but can you do better than to rely on the judgment of your elders and betters, educated men of good intent?

If there is some question about the salvation of infants, even the babies of the Elect, with stricter Calvinists dooming them to the easiest room in Hell, but with gentler ministers arguing that we do not know God's intent and that we can have (presumably God-given) hope of them being among those to bask in God's presence, then surely Cotton Mather, so very much God's chosen (except in a few black moments), can be sure that *his* children are his emissaries to God? And so his own Angel had assured him.

It is always the last step in Cotton Mather's tacit philosophy that upsets his later readers: from small points of style—two adjectives instead of one, the play on words doubly or triply developed—to more important issues of the multiplicity of publications and good deeds, even to the application of doctrine, with the somewhat un-answerable logic of a child, he argues that if some is good, more is better. Because he was so certain of his good intent, he rarely ap-proached and absolutely rejected any realization that the man who obviously goes too far (in the eyes of the world) in his efforts to reach a goal, especially an intangible or receding goal, will have his efforts greeted with mockery.

Cotton Mather may have deceived himself fairly steadily throughout his life that all he did was for God's glory, not his own pride. Nevertheless, he did realize from time to time that his best accomplishments were fly-specked with pride. And in his last hours he faced his failure: although he said that he had found the world "a very uneasy Wilderness" and longed to be with Christ, he recognized that his will was still strong; he struggled to the end to reach true Christian humility, his will "entirely swallowed up in the Will of God." Then, he reasoned, he would be with his Maker. He did not, however, lose his feeling of accomplishment. When his son asked for one last precept by which his father wished to be remembered, the answer was "Remember only that one word *Fruc-tuosus*." Certainly few men have labored as hard to be fruitful. He would have put first his efforts to preserve New England's Congregational churches, to keep alive the memory of the spirit and dedication of the first settlers, to "prove" that the new science only strengthened religion and belief in God. Later generations, with different values, might look with gentle eyes upon his advocacy of kindness to children, to the mentally ill, to the slave; his courageous attempt to preserve the lives of men, women, and children by preventive medicine; his careful plan for communal happiness with every man, according to his ability and place in life, doing good to all.

Notes and References

Chapter One

1. Eulogy in the *New England Weekly Journal*, February 19, 1728, reprinted in Abijah P. Marvin, *The Life and Times of Cotton Mather* (Boston, 1892), p. 572.

2. The primary sources for Cotton Mather's life are his *Diary*, edited by Worthington C. Ford, Massachusetts Historical Society *Collections*, 7th Series, Vols. VII - VIII (1911 - 1912; reprinted New York: Frederick Ungar, 1926, 1957), supplemented by the *Diary . . . for the Year 1712*, edited by William R. Manierre, II (Charlottesville, Virginia, 1964); and his unpublished autobiography, *Paterna*. A few added facts are in his son's dutiful biographical tribute: Samuel Mather, *The Life of the Very Reverend and Learned Cotton Mather, D.D. & F.R.S.* (Boston, 1729; facsimile reproduction, New York, 1970). To these biographical sources should be added Cotton Mather's letters, many of which are printed in Ford's edition of the *Diary* and in Kenneth Silverman, ed., *Selected Letters of Cotton Mather* (Baton Rouge, 1971). Many of his publications, including his sermons, are also remarkably revealing of their author inasmuch as he used for instructive purposes his own personal sorrows, his tribulations of various types, even his hard-earned practical wisdom.

Chapter Three

1. Johann Arndt (1555 - 1621), German mystic and early Pietist; his most influential book was *Vom wahren Christenthum* (True Christianity), the first part of which was printed in German in 1595, the whole in Latin in 1606 - 1609, and in English in 1712.

2. Hohann Gerhardt (1582 - 1637), German Lutheran theologian and pietist.

3. Philipp Jakob Spener (1635 - 1705), German theologian, called the father of pietism; his best known publication, *Pia Desideria*, was published in 1675 and has been frequently reprinted.

4. August Herman Francke (Franckius) (1663 - 1727), German pietist, very active and successful in organizing social and educational reforms.

5. For the influence of pietism on Cotton Mather, see Bibliography.

6. The question of Cotton Mather's membership in the Royal Society is resolved in George Lyman Kittredge, "Cotton Mather's Election into the Royal Society," *Publications*, Colonial Society of Massachusetts, XIV (1913), 81 - 114.

Chapter Four

1. Thomas J. Holmes, *Cotton Mather A Bibliography* (3 vols., Cambridge, Mass., 1940), a remarkably detailed, annotated bibliography with critical comments on the major works.

2. Examples of some types of Mather's sermons may be found in two reprints: George Harrison Orians, ed., *Days of Humiliation . . . Nine Sermons for Restoring Favor with an Angry God (1692 - 1727)* by Cotton Mather. Facsimile Reproductions (Gainesville, Fla., 1970); and A. W. Plumstead, ed., *The Wall and the Garden Selected Massachusetts Election Sermons 1670 - 1775* (Minneapolis, 1968) has Mather's Election Sermon of 1689, *The Way to Prosperity* (originally published Boston, 1690).

3. For critical estimates of *Pietas in Patrem*, see Kenneth B. Murdock, ed., *Selections from Cotton Mather* (New York, 1926), pp. xliv - xlviii; and Mark Van Doren, ed., *The Life of Sir William Phips* by Cotton Mather (New York, 1929), Preface.

4. Charles H. Lincoln, *Narratives of the Indian Wars 1675 - 1699* (New York, 1933), p. 177.

5. Cotton Mather, *Diary* (New York, 1957), Vol. I, 163, 166, 169 - 71.

6. At the Massachusetts Historical Society, Boston.

7. One hundred fifteen letters are printed with Mather's *Diary*; these were selected from the holdings of the Massachusetts Historical Society (over 100 manuscript letters) and of the American Antiquarian Society (over 300 items). Other libraries have lesser collections: see Holmes, *Cotton Mather A Bibliography*, Vol. III, 1301 - 1304. Individual letters also have been printed in various historical works; for a partial listing, see Holmes, Vol. II, 550 - 56. The most comprehensive collection of the letters is Kenneth B. Silverman, ed., *Selected Letters of Cotton Mather* (Baton Rouge, 1971); this prints or reprints, with some passages omitted, about four-fifths of the 569 extant letters. (Note: a number of Mather's publications entitled *A Letter* or *Letters* are not in the true sense letters, but are really timely essays; for example, a 1702 work, *A Letter to Ungospellized Plantations.*)

8. Manuscript volume, University of Virginia Library.

9. Massachusetts Historical Society *Collections*, 1825, series 3, vol. I, 126 - 33; reprinted in *The Andros Tracts* (Boston, 1869); reprinted with identification of the characters in Kenneth B. Murdock, ed., *Selections from Cotton Mather* (New York, 1926), pp. 363 - 71.

10. Four small volumes survive, at the American Antiquarian Society.

11. Twenty-three at the American Antiquarian Society, three at the Massachusetts Historical Society.

12. Some of his elegies and epitaphs have been reprinted in James F. Hunnewell, ed., III, IV *Early American Poetry. Elegies and Epitaphs, 1677 - 1717* (Boston, 1896). The most complete listing of Mather's verse (59 entries) is in Harold S. Jantz, *The First Century of New England Verse* (New York, 1943; reprinted 1962), pp. 227 - 34.

Chapter Five

1. Cotton Mather, *Diary of*, edited by Worthington C. Ford, *Collections of the Massachusetts Historical Society*, 7th ser., vols. VII - VIII (1911 - 1912); republished New York, 1926, 1957. Mr. Ford was an extremely unsympathetic editor, and his contempt for Mather and Mather's religious beliefs is very evident. Diaries for 1681, 1683, 1685, 1686, 1692, 1693, 1696, 1697, 1698, 1699, 1700, 1701, 1702, 1703, 1705, 1706, 1707, 1709, 1711, 1713, 1716, 1717, 1718, 1721, and 1724, plus some letters and lists of his sermon texts, were located and included in this two-volume work of over 1,400 pages. One additional year has also been printed: *The Diary of Cotton Mather D.D., F.R.S. for the Year 1712*, edited by William R. Manierre II (Charlottesville, Virginia, 1964).

2. Samuel Sewall, *Diary of . . . 1674 - 1729, Collections of Massachusetts Historical Society*, 5th ser., vols. V - VII (1878 - 1882). This, the best-known colonial diary, has been much reprinted in excerpts.

3. Barrett Wendell, *Cotton Mather The Puritan Priest* (New York, 1891, 1926, 1963).

Chapter Six

1. For a discussion of the Salem tragedy in the perspective of outbreaks of witchcraft in Europe, see George Lyman Kittredge, *Witchcraft in Old and New England* (New York, 1956).

2. Leading nineteenth-century accusers of the Mathers included Charles W. Upham, George H. Moore, and Brooks Adams; as late as 1921 J. T. Adams echoed them in *The Founding of New England*.

3. Among the nineteenth-century defenders of the Mathers were such scholars as Delano A. Goddard and William F. Poole; fair treatment also can be found in later books and articles by Barrett Wendell, Kenneth B. Murdock, Thomas J. Holmes, George Lyman Kittredge, and Samuel Eliot Morison.

4. The "cases"—that is, records of the trials— can be read in William Elliot Woodward, ed., *Records of Salem Witchcraft, Copied from the Original Documents* (Roxbury, Mass., 1864); five cases are also in David Levin, ed., *What Happened in Salem?* (New York, 1960).

5. Cotton Mather, *Things for a Distress'd People to Think Upon* (Boston, 1696), p. 27.

6. Cotton Mather, *Diary* (New York, 1957), Vol. I, 216.

7. Early protestors of the persecution of unfortunates as witches included Johann Wier (Weyer, Wierus) (1515 - 1588), *De Praestigiis Daemonum* (1563, with later enlarged editions); Reginald Scot (1538? - 1599), *Discoverie of Witchcraft* (1584); Thomas Hobbes (1588 - 1679), *Leviathan* (1651); John Webster (1610 - 1682), *The Displaying of Supposed Witchcraft* (1677); the most cogent and logical protest against the belief came just too late to help in the Salem troubles: Balthaser Bekker's *De*

Betoverde Weereld (The Enchanted World), published in 1691 and 1693. A brief discussion of this literature can be found in Kittredge, *Witchcraft in Old and New England*, pp. 338 - 57.

8. William Perkins (1558 - 1602), a much-respected authority for all Puritans, *A Discourse of the Damned Art of Witchcraft* (1608); Richard Bernard (c. 1568 - 1641), Puritan divine, *Guide to Grand Jurymen . . . in cases of Witchcraft* (1627, 1629). John Gaul(e) (fl. c. 1650), noted theologian, *Select Cases of Conscience, touching Witches and Witchcraft* (1646). Richard Baxter (1615 - 1691), an outstanding writer and authority on many religious questions, much respected by men of different churches, *The Certainty of the World of Spirits* (1691).

9. In Levin, *What Happened in Salem?*, pp. 139 - 41.

10. Cotton Mather, *Diary*, Vol. I, 216.

11. Ibid., Vol I, 163 - 64.

12. See Mather's Letter in the book written by his parishioners in his defense, *Some Few Remarks upon a Scandalous Book . . . by Robert Calef* (1701; also Mather's "Another Brand Pluckt out of the Burning," Section xii, reprinted in George Lincoln Burr, ed., *Narratives of the Witchcraft Cases* (New York, 1959), p. 320.

13. For his repeated protests against convicting the accused on spectral evidence alone, see his *Diary*, Vol. I, 150 - 51; *Wonders of the Invisible World* (Boston, 1693), pp. xvi - xvii: "Another Brand Pluckt out of the Burning," Section xii, in Robert Calef, *More Wonders of the Invisible World* (London, 1700), reprinted in Burr, *Narratives of the Witchcraft Cases*, p. 320; *Magnalia Christi Americana* (Hartford, 1855), Vol. II, 631; Letter, 4 Massachusetts Historical Society *Collections*, Vol. VIII.

14. His beliefs about witchcraft are stated in his publications on the subject, *passim;* and more concisely in "The Return of Several Ministers," printed in full in Increase Mather's *Cases of Conscience concerning Evil Spirits* (1693) and in part in Cotton Mather's *Wonders of the Invisible World* (1693); frequently reprinted; in full and with accuracy in Kenneth Murdock, *Increase Mather* (Cambridge, Mass., 1925), Appendix B. For Cotton Mather's statement that he wrote "The Return," see his Letter in *Some Few Remarks upon a Scandalous Book . . . by one Robert Calef* (1701).

15. Mather, *Diary*, Vol. I, 144 - 59.

16. *Diary*, Vol. I, 160 - 79.

17. *Diary*, Vol. I, 215.

18. For his Salem trips and charities, see his *Diary*, Vol. I, 204 - 205, 232, 271 - 72, 316, 363, 403, 476, 484, 521, 570, 581, 597; Vol. II, 111 - 13, 166, 361.

19. Published Boston, 1689; London, 1691, with a nine-page approving preface by Richard Baxter; Edinburgh, 1697; in a rewritten form in Mather's *Magnalia*, Book VI; in part in Burr, *Naratives of the Witchcraft Cases*, pp. 91 - 143.

20. Thomas J. Holmes, "Memorable Providences," in *Cotton Mather A Bibliography* (Cambridge, Mass., 1940), Vol. II, 658.

21. Published Boston, 1692, postdated 1693—2 imprints; London, 1693—3 editions, two of them abridged; Salem, 1861, abridged; London, 1862, 1865, c. 1874 (with 1862 date on title page), c. 1883 (with 1862 date on title page); Roxbury, Mass., 1866; in part, in Burr, *Narratives of the Witchcraft Cases*, pp. 209 - 51. For further bibliographical details, see Holmes, *Cotton Mather A Bibliography*, Vol. III, 1234 - 46.

22. Circulated in manuscript before March, 1693; published for the first time in Burr, *Narratives of the Witchcraft Cases*, pp. 253 - 87.

23. Circulated in manuscript after September, 1693; published without Cotton Mather's permission in Robert Calef, *More Wonders of the Invisible World* (London, 1700). Reprinted with *More Wonders*, Salem, 1796, 1823; Boston, 1828; reprinted with Cotton Mather's *Wonders of the Invisible World*, Salem, 1861; Boston, 1865; Roxbury, Mass., 1866; also in Henry Jones, *Strange Phenomena of New England* (New York, 1846); and in Burr, *Narratives of the Witchcraft Cases*, pp. 307 - 38. See Thomas J. Holmes, *The Surreptitious Printing of one of Cotton Mather's Manuscripts* in *Bibliographical Essays: A Tribute to Wilberforce Eames* (1924), issued separately (Cambridge, Mass., 1925); also Holmes, *Cotton Mather A Bibliography*, Vol. I, 45 - 47.

24. Mather, *Diary*, Vol. I, 173, 265; Mather, *Triumphs over Troubles* (1701), *passim*; also Holmes, *The Surreptitious Printing* (Cambridge, 1925), p. 4.

Chapter Seven

1. *Magnalia Christi Americana: Or, the Ecclesiastical History of New-England, From Its First Planting in the Year 1620. Unto the Year of our Lord, 1698* (London, 1702); reprinted, 2 volumes (Hartford, 1820); reprinted, 2 volumes (Hartford, 1853); reprinted in part a number of times, including Kenneth B. Murdock, ed., *Selections from Cotton Mather* (New York, 1926). Page references in this book are to the 1853 edition.

2. Cotton Mather, *Diary* (New York, 1957), Vol. I, 166. For a detailed account of the *Magnalia's* conception, growth, and publication, see Holmes, *Cotton Mather A Bibliography*, Vol. II, 583 - 86.

3. Mather, *Diary*, Vol. I, 424 - 26, 427, 445.

4. *The Bostonian Ebenezer* (1698).

5. Thomas Prince (1601? - 1673), governor of Plymouth Colony; not to be confused with the later, better-known Thomas Prince (1687 - 1758), clergyman and historian.

6. *Early Piety, Exemplified in the Life and Death of Mr. Nathanael Mather* (London, 1689; Boston, 1690).

7. *Brontologia Sacra: The Voice of the Glorious God in the Thunder* (London, 1695) and *Terribilia Dei Remarkable Judgments of God, on*

Several Sorts of Offenders, in Several Scores of Instances . . . Two Sermons (1697).

8. *Pillars of Salt. An History of Some Criminals Executed in this Land; For Capital Crimes. With some of their Dying Speeches; Collected and Published, For the Warning of such as Live in Destructive Courses of Ungodliness* (1699).

9. John Hale (1636 - 1700), first minister of Beverley, *A Modest Enquiry* (1702).

10. Mather, *Diary*, Vol. I, 369; Homes, *Cotton Mather: A Bibliography*, Vol. III, 369.

11. For an interesting and detailed analysis of Mather's style in the *Magnalia*, see Willima Reid Manierre II, "Verbal Patterns in Cotton Mather's *Magnalia*," *The Quarterly Journal of Speech*, Vol. XLVII (December 1961), 402 - 13.

12. Moses Coit Tyler, *A History of American Literature* (New York, 1878), Vol. II, 82 - 84.

13. Barrett Wendell, *Cotton Mather: The Puritan Priest* (New York, 1963), p. 118.

14. Murdock, *Selections from Cotton Mather*, p. xli.

15. Sacvan Bercovitch, "Cotton Mather," in Everett Emerson, ed., *Major Writers of Early American Literature* (Madison, 1972), pp. 141 - 49.

16. *New York Times*, Vol. CXXI, No. 38,555 (August 16, 1963), pp. 1, 22 - 24.

Chapter Eight

1. Cotton Mather, *Bonifacius. An Essay upon the Good*, edited with an Introduction by David Levin (Cambridge, Mass., 1966). All page references are to this edition, which follows the original text of 1710.

2. Revelation 21.

3. Limners were illustrators or drawers; scriveners were professional copyists; apothecaries prepared medicines. (One of Mather's daughters became skilled in the last of these trades.)

4. For other attacks on the slave trade, see Cotton Mather, *The Negro Christianized* (1706), pp. 23 - 27, and *Theopolis Americana* (1710), pp. 21 - 22.

5. For a very adequate discussion of the *Silence Dogood* papers, see Richard E. Amacher, *Benjamin Franklin* (Twayne, 1962), pp. 105 - 13.

6. For a discussion of the various editions, see Thomas J. Holmes, *Cotton Mather: A Bibliography* (Cambridge, Mass., 1940), Vol. I, 89 - 94, 324 - 38.

7. Benjamin Franklin, *Autobiographical Writings*, Selected and Edited by Carl Van Doren (New York, 1945), pp. 223, 604; see also pp. 629, 784, 256.

8. Moses Coit Tyler, *A History of American Literature* (New York, 1878), Vol. II, 84

9. Barrett Wendell, *Cotton Mather: The Puritan Priest* (New York, 1963), p. 221.

10. Holmes, *Cotton Mather: A Bibliography*, Vol. I, 92.

11. Arthur Bernon Tourtellot, "The Early Reading of Benjamin Franklin," *Harvard Library Bulletin*, Vol. XXIII (January 1975), 5 - 41.

Chapter Nine

1. Reprinted, with the style modernized, Charleston, Mass., 1815; reprinted in part in Kenneth B. Murdock, *Selections from Cotton Mather* (New York, 1926), pp. 285 - 362. The Facsimile Reproduction of the 1721 edition, with an introduction by Josephine K. Peircy, (Gainesville, Fla., 1968) is the edition used for this chapter. For the question of the date of publication, see Holmes, *Cotton Mather A Bibliography*, Vol. I, 129; also G. L. Kittredge, Colonial Society of Massachusetts *Publications*, Vol. XIV (1911), 98 - 99.

2. For American Deism, especially in relation to Cotton Mather, see Woodbridge Riley, *American Thought from Puritanism to Pragmatism and Beyond* (New York, 1923); also Riley, *American Philosophy The Early Schools* (New York, 1958), pp. 191 - 320.

3. James Usher or Ussher (1581 - 1656), Irish scholar and historian, Bishop of Meath, Archbishop of Armagh; known for his belief in tolerance and his efforts at reconciliation between Churchmen and Dissenters; *A Body of Divinity* (1645).

4. Hugo Grotius (1583 - 1645), Dutch jurist and theologian; supporter of moderation in theological disputes; *De Veritate Religiones Christianae* (1622).

5. Johann Heinrich Alsted (1588 - 1638), German theologian and philosopher; *Scientiarum Omnium Encyclopaedia.*

6. Hermannus Witsius (1636 - 1708), Dutch theologian; much respected by Puritans for his basic work on Covenant theology, *De Oeconomia foederum Dei cum hominibus* (1677); translated into English, *The Economy of the Covenants between God and Man* (1693).

7. Richard Baxter (1615 - 1691), English Presbyterian clergyman with ecumenical views; voluminous writer; *The Saints' Everlasting Rest* (1650), *Reliquiae Baxterianae* (1696).

8. For a detailed discussion of the Chain of Being, see Arthur O. Lovejoy, *The Great Chain of Being* (New York, 1960).

9. For evaluations of *The Christian Philosopher* in the history of science, see Theodore Hornberger, "Notes on *The Christian Philosopher,*" in Holmes, *Cotton Mather: A Bibliography*, Vol. I, 133 - 37; and Otho T. Beal, Jr., and Richard H. Shryock, *Cotton Mather, First Significant Figure in American Medicine* (Baltimore, 1954), pp. 50 - 52.

10. For an appreciation of Mather's literary artistry in *The Christian Philosopher*, see Murdock, *Selections from Cotton Mather*, Introduction, pp. lii - liv.

Chapter Ten

1. Mather always uses "parable" in what is now the obsolete sense of easily procurable or prepared, get-at-able.

2. Only one chapter of *The Angel of Bethesda* was published during Mather's lifetime. Despite his efforts to have the work published, loyally followed by his son Samuel's efforts after his father's death, the *Angel* remained in manuscript (in the American Antiquarian Society Library) until lengthy sections of it were published in Otho T. Beall, Jr., and Richard H. Shryock, *Cotton Mather, First Significant Figure in American Medicine* (Baltimore, 1954), pp. 127 - 234. Eighteen years later the whole surviving manuscript was published, Gordon W. Jones, M.D., ed., *The Angel of Bethesda, An Essay Upon the Common Maladies of Mankind* (Barre, Mass., 1972). Dr. Jones's valuable footnotes identify many of Mather's sources and explain many of the cures.

3. Ola Elizabeth Winslow, *A Destroying Angel: The Conquest of Smallpox in Colonial Boston* (Boston, 1974), pp. 38 - 43.

4. Letter to John Winthrop, December 26, 1720, in Kenneth Silverman, ed., *Selected Letters of Cotton Mather* (Baton Rouge, 1971), p. 332.

5. Cotton Mather tells his readers that for the first capsula he is using his *Mens Sana in Corpore Sano. A Discourse upon Recovery from Sickness. Directing How Natural Health, may be Improved into Spiritual* (Boston, 1698).

6. Published as *The Angel of Bethesda* (New London, 1722).

7. For variations in this "third man" theory, see Lester S. King, *The Road to Medical Enlightenment 1650 - 1695* (London and New York, 1970), *passim*.

8. There are forty such capsulas in the printed *Angel*. Five capsulas are missing from Mather's manuscript; judging from the table of contents, at least four of these treated specific diseases and can be presumed to follow the basic pattern.

9. After Harvey's discovery of the circulation of the blood (published in 1628) there was great interest in the possible benefits of blood transfusion, including the use of animal blood.

10. Excrement of all types (bird, animal, human) was one of the commonest ingredients in early folk medicine. It is now known that urine does have some antiseptic value (and has been used or at least recommended for use on battlefields); feces and dung have some mineral content which might have helped in some illnesses.

11. Mather's "victorious remedy" is taken from John Colbatch, *Dissertation upon Mistletoe, a remedy in convulsive distemper*, a recent publication that Mather owned; Dr. Jones feels that Mather overestimated Colbatch's reputation as a physician.

12. Cotton Mather had his daughter the beloved (and intelligent) Katy,

trained so that she could do this, i.e., help the needy sick by dispensing herbs and other cures to them.

13. Mather was using a well-known book on industrial medicine, *De Morbis Articficium* (Modena, 1700), by Bernardino Ramazzini (1633 - 1717).

14. The more valuable secondary accounts of the inoculation controversy and Cotton Mather's part in it include: George Lyman Kittredge, "Some Lost Works of Cotton Mather," in *Mass. Hist. Soc. Proceedings*, XLV (1912), 418 - 79—an early study that opened the field for later investigation; John B. Blake, "The Inoculation Controversy in Boston, 1721 - 1722," *New England Quarterly*, XXV (1952), 489 - 506; Beall and Shryock, *Cotton Mather, First Significant Figure in American Medicine*—a detailed account; Raymond Phineas Stearns, *Science in the British Colonies* (Urbana, Ill., 1970), pp. 417 - 26; Winslow, *A Destroying Angel.* As the events of 1721 - 1722 called forth a pamphlet war, there are a number of primary accounts, including seven by Cotton Mather. These contemporary arguments, for and against inoculation, can be found through Kittredge's "Some Lost Works," Winslow's *Destroying Angel*, pp. 78 - 87, and Holmes's Bibliography (see "Smallpox" in the index).

15. Emanuele Timoni (Timonius), a Greek physician, educated at Padua and Oxford, member of the Royal Society; his account of the use of inoculation in Turkey was written late in 1713 and published in the *Philosophical Transactions* of the Royal Society in 1714. Giacomo Pilarino (Jacobus Pylarinus), another Greek physician, published *Nova et Tute Variolas Excitande per Transplantationem Methodus* (A new and safe method of causing smallpox by transplantation) in Venice, 1715; his account appeared in the *Transactions* in 1717.

16. This attempt at a reasoned explanation for the success of inoculation, together with his recognition that the virus was composed of living organisms, makes Cotton Mather "the outstanding medical thinker" in colonial America, according to Beall and Shryock, pp. 113 - 17; cf. Stearns, p. 426.

17. For later use of the Boston experience as proof of the success and safety of inoculation, see Beall and Shryock, pp. 119 - 21; for a brief discussion of inoculation as the forerunner of vaccination (1798), also see Beall and Shryock, pp. 121 - 22.

18. Nicholas Culpeper (1616 - 1654), an apothecary turned physician, and a firm believer in astrology; his popular *The English Physician Enlarged* (London, 1653) had many reprintings, including a New England edition in 1708.

19. Beall and Shryock raise the question of whether the book failed to reach publication because of its confusion of purpose (in appealing to two different audiences).

Chapter Eleven

1. Mather, *Diary*, II, 733, 749, 774.

2. Boston, 1726; reprinted, New York, 1938. For a detailed account of Mather's many scholarly and historical references in the *Manuductio*, see Kennerly M. Woody, "Bibliographical Notes to Cotton Mather's *Manuductio ad Ministerium*," *Early American Literature*, Vol. VI, Supplement, pp. 1 - 98.

3. David Chytraeus (1531 - 1600), *Oratio de Studio Theologiae* (Wittenberg, 1581). Chytraeus, sometimes regarded as an early Pietist, advocated that the study of theology should be marked by the practice of piety, not by the strife of disputation.

4. St. Gregory I (ca. 540 - 604), *Cura Pastoralis.*

5. Translated by Hugh Walford in *Dr. Cotton Mather's Student and Preacher* (London, 1789).

6. Johann Heinrich Alsted (1588 - 1638), German theologian and philosopher; *Scientiarum Omnium Encyclopaedia.*

7. Samuel Eliot Morison, *The Founding of Harvard College* (Cambridge, Mass., 1935), pp. 434 - 36; Perry Miller and Thomas H. Johnson, *The Puritans* (New York, 1938), pp. 698, 703 - 704.

8. Among them John Milton (1608 - 1674), *Artis Logicae Plenior Institutio* (1672), a digest of Ramean logic and so in opposition to the traditional Aristotelian concepts.

9. Mather notes particularly Johannes Maccovius (Makowski) (1588 - 1644), a Polish theologian and author of *Metaphysica* (Amsterdam, 1651).

10. William Ames (1576 - 1633), Puritan divine; *Medulla Theologiae* (1642).

11. Henry More (1614 - 1687), theologian, leader of the Cambridge Platonists; *Enchiridion Ethicum Praecipua Moralis* (1679, 1695).

12. Johann Arndt (1555 - 1621), German mystic and early pietist; *Vom wahren Christenthum* (True Christianity), first part published in German, 1595; the whole translated into Latin, 1606 - 1609; into English, 1712.

13. Mather objects by name to three satirists of some note: Samuel Butler (1612 - 1680), author of *Hudibras* (1663, 1664, 1678), a mock-heroic poem that ridicules Puritans; Edward (Ned) Ward (1667 - 1731), whose coarsely humorous attacks on Puritans include *A Trip to New England* (1699) and *Hudibras Redivivus* (1705 - 1707); and Thomas Brown (1663 - 1704), a well-known wit in his day, whose works were published posthumously as *Dialogues, Essays, Declamations, Satires* (1707).

14. Sir Richard Blackmore (c. 1650 - 1729), physician and voluminous poet, of considerable prominence in his day; *Prince Arthur* (1695), *King Arthur* (1697), *The Creation* (1712).

15. Mather shows his reading of *Paradise Lost* in the *Magnalia Christi Americana* (1855 ed.), I, 183; II, 566 - 68.

16. Sir Isaac Newton (1642 - 1727), scientist, mathematician,

philosopher, president of the Royal Society; *Philosophiae Naturalis Principia Mathematica* (1687).

17. Robert Boyle (1627 - 1691), natural philosopher, chemist, theologian, one of the founders of the Royal Society; *Usefulness of Experimental Natural Philosophy* (1663); *The Christian Virtuoso* (1690).

18. John Ray (1627 - 1705), naturalist and botanist, Fellow Royal Society; *The Wisdom of God Manifested in the Works of the Creation* (1691).

19. Thomas Fuller (1608 - 1661), clergyman and historian: *A Pisgah—Sight of Palestine and the Confines Thereof* (1650).

20. William Camden (1551 - 1623), antiquarian and historian; *Britannia* (1586, 1607), translated into English by Philemon Holland in 1610.

21. John Oldmixon (1673 - 1742), journalist; *The British Empire in America* (1708).

22. Especially recommended: Matthias Prideaux (1622 - 1646?), Royalist writer and historian; *Easy and Compendious Introduction for the Reading all sorts of Histories* (1648, and frequently reprinted).

23. Especially recommended: James Howell (1594? - 1666), Welsh Royalist writer; *Epistolae Ho-elianae: Familiar Letters* (4 vols., 1645 - 1655, and frequently reprinted). Also, Samuel von Pufendorf or Puffendorf (1632 - 1694), German jurist and historian; *De jure naturae et gentium* (1672) is considered his master work.

24. Anthony à Wood (1632 - 1695), English antiquarian; *Athenae Oxonieses* (1691 - 92, 1721).

25. Gilbert Burnet (1643 - 1715), Bishop of Salisbury; *The History of the Reformation of the Church of England* (1679, 1681, 1714).

26. Samuel Clarke (1599 - 1683), English divine; *Lives of Sundry Eminent Persons* (1683). The Mathers were dissatisfied with his life of Richard Mather.

27. Matthew Poole (1624 -`1709), Presbyterian divine and Bible commentator; *Synopsis Criticorum* (1669 - 76); *Annotations upon the Holy Bible* (1688). Matthew Henry (1662 - 1714), Nonconformist minister and Bible commentator; *An Exposition of the Old and New Testaments* (1708 - 10). The commentaries of these two scholars are still standard works of reference.

28. Theodoret (390 - 457), Bishop of Cyrrhus, Greek theologian, church historian, Bible commentator, and exegete.

29. St. John Chrysostum (347 - 407), Greek father, Archbishop of Constantinople; famed for his preaching.

30. St. Augustine (354 - 430), church father, Bishop of Hippo (northern Africa); *Confessiones* (397); *De Civitate Dei* (426).

31. Mather, *The Diary of . . . for the Year 1717*, ed. by William R. Manierre II (Charlottesville, Va., 1964), p. 97.

32. Other expressions of Cotton Mather's belief in tolerance and his desire for an ecumenical spirit among Protestants may be seen in his *Diary*, Vol. I, 149, Vol. II, 530 - 31, 535 - 38; *Magnalia Christi Americana* (1702),

Vol. I, 243, Vol. II, 525; *Optanda: Good Men Described* (1692); *Theopolis Americana* (1710); *The Stone Cut out of the Mountain* (1716); *Malachi. Or, The Everlasting Gospel, Preached unto the Nations* (1717); *Piety and Equity, United* (1717); *Brethren Dwelling Together in Unity* (1718); *Letter to John Shute Barrington* (1719); *Three Letters from New England* (1721); *Vital Christianity* (1725).

33. St. Thomas Aquinas (c. 1225 - 1274), Italian theologian and scholastic philosopher; *Summa Theologiae* (1267 - 1273).

34. St. Thomas à Kempis (c. 1380 - 1471), German mystic; *De Imitatione Christi* (1486).

35. Johann Gerhard (1582 - 1637), prominent German Lutheran theologian; Philipp Jakob Spener (1635 - 1705), German theologian, called the father of German Pietism; Gisbert Voetius (1589 - 1676), Dutch theologian.

36. Franklin, *Autobiographical Writings*, pp. 632 - 33; also p. 256.

37. Moses Coit Tyler, *A History of American Literature* (New York, 1878), Vol. II, 84 - 87.

38. Kenneth B. Murdock, Introduction to *Selections from Cotton Mather* (New York, 1926), p. xxxiii.

39. Perry Miller, "A Note on the Manuductio ad Ministerium," in Thomas J. Holmes, *Cotton Mather, A Bibliography* (Cambridge, Mass., 1940), Vol. II, pp. 630 - 35. The section of the *Manuductio* on poetry with its digression on style is reprinted in Miller and Johnson, *The Puritans* pp. 684 - 89, with the comment that it is the best essay on style written in the American colonies. See also Eugene R. White, "Cotton Mather's *Manuductio ad Ministerium*," in the *Quarterly Journal of Speech*, Vol. XLIX (1963), 308 - 19. For an important discussion of the influence of German pietism and the practices of the University of Halle on Mather's suggested curriculum, see Kennerly M. Woody, "Cotton Mather's *Ministerium ad Theologium:* The 'More Quiet and Hopeful Way,' " in *Early American Literature*, Vol. IV, No. 2, pp. 3 - 48.

Chapter Twelve

1. The fascination of two-headed snakes has lasted: in 1974 the zoo in Los Angeles reported itself as having one, and local newspapers throughout the country printed the story and picture.

Selected Bibliography

PRIMARY SOURCES

Cotton Mather's printed works include 468 items; a number of unpublished items, ranging from letters and notebooks to long treastises, remain in manuscript. The most complete listing is to be found in Thomas James Holmes's *Cotton Mather A Bibliography of His Works*, 3 vols. (Cambridge, Mass.): Harvard University Press, 1940. This comprehensive work is far more than an annotated bibliography: rarer items usually are summarized, and important works are discussed in essays by outstanding scholars.

In the following selection of Mather's works, the asterisked titles are translated after the listing of his works.

1. The More Important Publications, Illustrative of His Varied Output; All Are Available in Reprint
The Angel of Bethesda. An Essay upon the Common Maladies of Mankind. Completed in 1724. Edited by Gordon W. Jones, M.D. Barre (Mass.), 1972.
*Bonifacius.** An Essay Upon the Good, that is to be Devised and Designed, by Those Who Desire to Answer the Great End of Life, and to do Good while they Live. Boston, 1710. Reprinted, complete or in part, at least nineteen times in the nineteenth century, under the popular title *Essays to do Good;* reprinted, edited by and with a valuable introduction by David Levin. Cambridge (Mass.): Belknap Press, 1966; facsimile reproduction, with an introduction by Josephine K. Piercy, Gainesville (Fla.): Scholars' Facsimiles & Reprints, 1967.
The Christian Philosopher: A Collection of The Best Discoveries in Nature, With Religious Improvements. London, 1721, facsimile reproduction with an introduction by Josephine K. Piercy, Gainesville (Fla.): Scholars' Facsimiles & Reprints, 1968. Also reprinted in part in Kenneth B. Murdock, ed. *Selections from Cotton Mather*, pp. 285 - 362. New York: Harcourt, Brace, 1926 (reprinted Hafner, 1960).
*Curiosa Americana.** 82 letters, 1712 - 1724, prepared by Cotton Mather for the Royal Society of London. Some were printed and some were excerpted and printed in the *Philosophical Transactions* of the Royal Society; some were circulated in manuscript; some have disappeared. Some were published by Mather separately and / or in longer works;

for example, his letter to the Society, "Way of Proceeding in the Small-Pox Inoculated in New England," became his *An Account of the Method and Success of Inoculating the Small-Pox* (London, 1722) and the Appendix to Chapter XX of *The Angel of Bethesda; his letter on the Nishmath-Chajim** was separately published in *The Angel of Bethesda* (New London, 1722) and as Chapter V in the longer *Angel of Bethesda* (1972). *Vide infra,* G. L. Kittredge (Biographical and Critical Studies).

Days of Humilitation Times of Affliction and Disaster. Nine Sermons for Restoring Favor with an Angry God (1696 - 1727). Facsimile Reproductions, with an Introduction by George Harrison Orians. Gainesville (Fla.): Scholars' Facsimiles & Reprints, 1970. Nine examples of Cotton Mather's use throughout his preaching career of natural phenomena (rainbows, storms, earthquakes), catastrophes (fire), and threatened catastrophes (defeat of England by France) to urge people to reform. "Things for a Distress'd People to Think Upon," his Election Sermon of 1696, and "Advice from the Watch Tower" (1713) offer especially vivid pictures of the evils of the day. "A Voice from Heaven" (1719) is not a sermon, at least in its published form, but is Mather's account of the Aurora Borealis, December 17, 1719.

Decennium Luctuosum.* An History of Remarkable Occurrences, In the Long War, . . . with the Indian Salvages From the Year, 1688, To the Year, 1698. Boston, 1699. Reprinted as an appendix to Book Vii, *Magnalia Christi Americana,* London, 1702; Hartford, 1820, 1853. Also reprinted with footnotes in Charles H. Lincoln, ed., *Narratives of the Indian Wars 1675 - 1699,* pp. 179 - 300. New York: Scribner's, 1913. Often considered the most successful of Cotton Mather's histories.

Diary of. Ed. Worthington C. Ford, Massachusetts Historical Society *Collections,* 7th Series, vols. VII - VIII (1911 - 1912). Reprinted New York: Frederick Ungar, 1926, 1957. (Ford's obvious contempt for Puritanism and for Cotton Mather has been criticised by later critics as his bias is very evident in his preface and in many of his footnotes.)

Diary of . . . For the Year 1712. Ed. William R. Manierre, II. Charlottesville: University of Virginia, 1964. Supplies, from a later found manuscript, a year that is missing in Ford's edition.

Magnalia Christi Americana:* Or, The Ecclesiastical History of New-England, from . . . 1620, unto . . . 1698. London, 1702. Reprinted, 2 vols., Hartford: Silas Andrus, 1820; reprinted, 2 vols., with Introduction and Notes (including translations) by Rev. Thomas Robbins, Hartford: Silas Andrus & Son, 1853; reprinted, Edited and Abridged by Raymond J. Cunningham, New York: F. Ungar, 1970. Also reprinted in part, Murdock, *Selections,* pp. 1 - 148.

Manuductio ad Ministerium.* Directions for a Candidate of the Ministry.

Boston, 1726. Reprinted in facsimile with a Bibliographical Note by Thomas J. Holmes and Kenneth B. Murdock. New York: Facsimile Text Society (Columbia University Press), 1938.

Memorable Providences, Relating to Witchcrafts and Possessions. Boston, 1689; also London, 1691 (with preface by the noted Richard Baxter); also Edinburgh, 1697. Reprinted in part in George L. Burr, ed. *Narratives of the Witchcraft Cases,* pp. 91 - 143. New York: Scribner's, 1914 (reprinted Barnes and Noble, 1959).

*Pietas in Patriam:** *The Life and Death of His Excellency Sir William Phips, Knt.* London, 1697. Reprinted by the author in his *Magnalia Christi Americana,* Book ii (1702, 1820, 1853, 1967). Reprinted in Murdock's *Selections,* pp. 149 - 283; also reprinted with the title *The Life of Sir William Phips,* edited by and with a preface by Mark Van Doren. New York: Covici-Friede, 1929.

"Political Fables," manuscript circulated c. 1692, first printed in 1825; reprinted, with author identification, 1869. Reprinted, Murdock's *Selections,* pp. 363 - 71, with identification of the characters in the four fables.

Selected Letters of. Compiled with Commentary by Kenneth Silverman. Baton Rouge: Louisiana State University Press, 1971. About four-fifths of Mather's extant letters, including letters to the Royal Society.

Selections from. Edited with an Introduction and Notes by Kenneth B. Murdock. New York: Harcourt, Brace, 1926; reprinted New York: Hafner Publishing Co., 1960. Includes, with very helpful notes, sections of the *Magnalia Christi Americana* and of *The Christian Philosopher;* and complete reprintings of *The Life of Sir William Phips,* the Political Fables, and a letter to Dr. Woodward (one of Mather's contributions to the Royal Society).

The Wonders of the Invisible World, Observations As well Historical as Theological, upon the Nature, the Number, and the Operations of the Devils. . . . Boston, 1692 (postdated 1693). Also printed, abridged, in London, 1693, with the title: *The Wonders of the Invisible World; Being an Account of the Tryals of Several Witches, Lately Executed in New-England: and of several remarkable Curiosities therein Occurring.* Reprinted a number of times during the mid years of the nineteenth century in England and Massachusetts, with Increase Mather's *Cases of Conscience* or with Robert Calef's *More Wonders of the Invisible World;* of these editons, Samuel Gardner Drake's *The Witchcraft Delusion in New England,* Roxbury (Mass.), 1866, has been reprinted, New York: B. Franklin, 1970. Also reprinted in part in George Lincoln Burr, ed. *Narratives of the Witchcraft Cases,* pp. 209 - 51. New York: Scribner's, 1914 (reprinted Barnes & Noble, 1959).

2. Other Publications of Special Interest

*Agricola.** *Or, the Religious Husbandman: The Main Intentions of*

Religion, Served in the Business and Language of Husbandry. Boston, 1727; reprinted, Mason I. Lowance, Jr., ed. New York, 1971. Addressed to the farmers, still the most numerous class in New England society, this late and ambitious work uses the imagery of farming (plowing, sowing, mowing, harvesting, etc.) to clarify the Calvinist religious experience; interspersed with short, devotional songs.

A Brand Pluck'd Out of the Burning. Circulated in manuscript in 1692. Printed in George Lincoln Burr, ed. *Narratives of the Witchcraft Cases 1648 - 1706*, pp. 253 - 87. New York: Scribner's, 1914; Barnes and Noble, 1959. The Mercy Short case.

Another Brand Pluckt out of the Burning. Circulated in manuscript in 1693. Printed surreptitiously in Robert Calef. *More Wonders of the Invisible World.* London, 1700; Salem, 1795, 1823; Boston, 1828; reprinted with Cotton Mather's *Wonders of the Invisible World*, Salem, 1861; Boston [1865]; Roxbury (Mass.), [1866]; in Burr, *Narratives*, pp. 307 - 23. The Margaret Rule case. These accounts of two Boston witchcraft cases indicate clearly Mather's beliefs about witchcraft and the treatment he advocated for the bewitched.

Concio ad Populum.* *A Distressed People Entertained with Proposals for the Relief of their Distresses.* Boston, 1719. Advice to Bostonians in a year of business depression: form associations (to advise and help each other), be frugal, be industrious.

Corderius Americanus.* *An Essay upon The Good Education of Children.* Boston, 1708; Boston, [1774]; Boston, 1828; reprinted as "Cotton Mather's Tribute to Ezekiel Cheever." Boston: *Old South Leaflets,* No. 177 [n.d.].

The Deplorable State of New-England, By Reason of a Covetous and Treacherous Governour, and Pusillanimous Counsellors. London, 1708; Boston, 1721; Boston: Mass. Hist. Soc. *Collections,* 5th series, VI (1879), 97 - 131. One of Mather's political publications, an attack on the corrupt practices of Governor Dudley, who he accused of accepting bribery, refusing to appoint judges, and trading with the enemy. (A slightly earlier pamphlet, *A Memorial Of the Present Deplorable State of New England* [London, 1707], supported Mather's charges by affidavits from a number of New Englanders.)

Fair Weather. Or Considerations to Dispel the Clouds, & Allay the Storms, of Discontent. Boston, 1692. A protest against New England's sins: Pride, Gluttony, Drunkenness, Wantonness; followed by a tirade against Indians, "those Tawney Pagans, than which there are not worse Divels Incarnate upon Earth," occasioned by the murder of the Reverend Shubael Dummer of York, Maine.

The Faith of the Fathers. Or, The Articles of the True Religion, All of them Exhibited In the Express Words of the Old Testament. Boston, 1699. One of Mather's numerous catechisms, but of special interest as all the answers are from the Old Testament, with the double purpose of confirming Christians in their faith and of converting the Jewish nation.

Family-Religion, Excited and Assisted. [Boston, 1705]; Boston, 1707; London, [1709], 1713; Boston, 1714 (revised, with an Indian translation); Boston, 1720, 1727; Newport, [1740]; Boston, 1747. Mather always was greatly concerned about prayerless homes; this little book of instruction became one of his most popular offerings.

A Family Well-Ordered. Or An Essay to Render Parents and Children Happy in one another. Boston, 1699. Duties of parents to children and children to parents, plus a plea for more village schools, better attended.

La Fe del Christiano: En Veyntequatro Articulos de la Institucion de Christo.* Boston, 1699. Translated with an introduction and notes by Thomas E. Johnston, *Early American Literature Newsletter*, Vol. II, No. 2 (Fall 1967), 7 - 21. Mather learned Spanish in three weeks in order to convert the Catholic West Indies.

The Fisher-mans Calling. Boston, 1712. A plea for good treatment of fishermen by the owners of fishing fleets serves as an introduction to a sermon addressed to the "Brethren of Low Degree." Also of interest for the nature passages: the bountiful wonders of the sea lead Mather to praise the "Glorious Father of Nature."

Une Grande Voix du Ciel a la France.* Boston, 1725. An effort, in French, to strengthen the Protestant church in France, followed by criticism of the Roman Catholic religion.

The Heavenly Conversation. An Essay Upon the Methods of Conversing With a Glorious Christ, in Every Step of our Life. Boston, 1710. The author recognizes that the faith and practice he is preaching is "true American Pietism."

Lex Mercatoria.* *Or, The Just Rules of Commerce Declared.* Boston, 1705. On false dealing (dishonesty): New Englanders, as high professors of religion, are honest, virtuous, and industrious, but there are some "horrid Cheats" pulling them down.

Little Flocks Guarded against Grievous Wolves. Boston, 1691. A warning against the heresies and blasphemies of Quakerism.

Malachi.* *Or, The Everlasting Gospel, Preached unto the Nations.* Boston, 1717; Philadelphia, 1767. The broad principles upon which all churches should unite—Mather's ecumenical spirit at its best.

A Midnight Cry. An Essay For our Awakening out of that Sinful Sleep, To which we are at This Time too much disposed. Boston, 1692. Interesting for Mather's strong belief (in the 1690s) that the Second Coming of Christ was near at hand for his hope of being a second Calvin or even a second John the Baptist.

The Negro Christianized. An Essay to Excite and Assist that Good Work, The Instruction of Negro-Servants in Christianity. Boston, 1706. Intended for every family in New England that had Negroes in it and for the slave-owners of the Indies.

*Parentator.** *Memoirs of Remarkables in the Life and the Death of the Ever-Memorable Dr. Increase Mather.* Boston, 1724. A long (24 pages of introduction, 239 pages of text) but readable biographical tribute.

Pascentius. A very brief Essay upon The Methods of Piety. Boston, 1714. Advice in "hard Times": Banish fear, the fear of want, an epidemical "distemper."

The Present State of New-England. Considered in a Discourse on the Necessities and Advantages of a Public Spirit In Every Man. Boston, 1690. Reprinted New York: Haskell House, 1972. A Thursday lecture sermon, delivered in response to reports of new invasions by the Indians and French on the northern settlements, urging the people to turn away God's wrath by strict enforcement of the laws against vice, debauchery, and profaneness.

*Psalterium Americanum.** *The Book of Psalms, In a Translation Exactly conformed unto the Original; but all in Blank Verse.* Boston, 1718. First extensive use of unrhymed verse in New England; the preface is of interest for Cotton Mather's literary theories.

The Quickened Soul. A Short and Plain Essay on, The Withered Hand Revived & Restored. Boston, 1720. Mather's mature belief (and teaching) concerning Election and Predestination: a man's desire to be of the Elect is indicative that he is of the Elect.

*Ratio Disciplinae Fratrum Nov Anglorum.** *A Faithful Account of the Discipline Professed and Practised; in the Churches of New-England.* Boston, 1726 (originally written in 1701; revised 1713 - 1719). Regarded by Mather and his contemporaries as one of his important services, and in use in Congregational churches throughout the eighteenth century.

Reason Satisfied: and Faith Established. Boston, 1712. One of three essays (*Reasonable Religion,* Boston, 1700; London, 1713; *A Man of Reason,* Boston, 1718) on the relation of reason and faith; against the spreading deism of the period, even though there are signs of deistic thinking in his own writing.

The Return of Several Ministers Consulted by His Excellency . . . Upon the Present Witchcrafts in Salem-Village. Boston, June 16, 1692. Printed in the Postscript of Increase Mather's *Cases of Conscience Concerning Evil Spirits.* Boston, 1693. Reprinted (entire, in part, or summarized) at least fifteen times by 1892; see Holmes, *Bibliography,* III, 910 - 14. Written by Cotton Mather but representing the general viewpoint of the clergy, this much- criticized advice to Governor Phips urges caution against credulity, the rejection of special evidence, and "exceeding tenderness" to those accused, but also urges "speedy and vigorous" prosecution of those guilty.

The Right Way to Shake off a Viper. An Essay, on a Case, Too Commonly calling for Consideration. What shall Good Men do, when they are Evil Spoken of? London, 1711; Boston, 1720. The author had the comfort of reporting that St. Paul, Beza, and Calvin in their times had been his fellow victims of calumny.

The Salvation of the Soul Considered. Boston, 1720. According to the critical judgment of Holmes (*Bibliography*, II, 950), the most moving and exalting of all of Cotton Mather's publications.

Some Considerations on the Bills of Credit Now Passing in New-England. Boston, 1691; reprinted in Andrew McFarland Davis, ed. *Tracts Relating to the Currency of the Massachusetts Bay 1682 - 1720.* Boston and New York: Houghton, Mifflin, 1902, pp. 13 - 21; also reprinted in Andrew McFarland Davis, ed. *Colonial Currency Reprints 1682 - 1751.* Boston: Prince Society, 1910, pp. 189 - 96. Urges the acceptance of paper money.

The Stone Cut out of the Mountain. And The Kingdom of God, in Those Maxims of it, that cannot be shaken. Printed with a Latin text, for international distribution, and sometimes referred to by the Latin title, *Lapis e Monte Excisus.* [Boston], 1716. One of Mather's favorite publications; he is speaking for one church, without schisms caused by foolish contentions about "Lesser Points, the Indifferents, or the Unnecessaries of Religion."

Theopolis Americana.* An Essay on the Golden Street Of the Holy City: Publishing, A Testimony against the Corruptions of the Market-Place. With Some Good Hopes of Better Things to be yet seen in the American World. Boston, 1710. This lengthy sermon gives a remarkably detailed picture of Mather's world of 1710 as he condemns dishonesty in many forms, including adulteration of wares, the abuse of the ignorant, breaking of contracts, robbing the public treasury; also points out the sin of the slave trade, abuse of Negroes (in keeping them from Christianity), mistreatment of Christianized Indians; notes the evil of rum drinking; admits the present regret for earlier persecution for religious differences and for the errors of the witch trials of 1692. But Mather is hopeful for the defeat of evil and that the Millennium is at hand, with America the likely site of the New Jerusalem.

A Token, for the Children of New-England, Or, Some Examples of Children, In whom the Fear of God was Remarkably Budding, before they Dyed. Boston, 1700 (printed with James Janeway's *Token for Children*). An example of a type of publication much favored by Mather; that such tales of early piety were generally popular is attested to by the repeated publication of *The Token* during the eighteenth century (see Holmes, III, 1104 - 14).

Vital Christianity: A Brief Essay On the Life of God, in the Soul of Man. [Philadelphia], 1725; Philadelphia, 1730; Boston, 1741. Cotton Mather's reconciliation with the beliefs of the Friends, even while he maintained his Calvinist views.

The Way to Prosperity. A Sermon Preached to the Honourable Convention Of the Governour, Council and Representatives. . . . Boston, 1689.

Reprinted in A. W. Plumstead, ed. *The Wall and the Garden Selected Massachusetts Election Sermons 1670 - 1775*, pp. 109 - 39. Minneapolis: University of Minnesota Press, 1968. The first of Mather's four Election Day sermons, interesting as a plea for peace between the colony's disputing political factions and as a call for support of schools in every town.

The Wonderful Works of God Commemorated. Boston, 1690. This sermon and his essay *Winter-Meditations* (Boston, 1693) are evidence of Mather's early interest in many aspects of nature and in natural science; both publications are forerunners of his *Christian Philosopher* (1721).

3.   Title Translations

Agricola—the farmer.

Bonifacius—doer of good.

Concio ad Populum—a discourse to the people.

Corderius Americanus—the American Cordier: Mathurin Cordier (1479 - 1564), the much-respected teacher of Calvin.

Curiosa Americana—American curiosities.

Decennium Luctuosum—ten years of sorrow.

La Fe del Christiano: En Veyntequatro Articulos de la Institucion de Christo—the faith of a Christian: the institutes of Christianity in twenty-four articles.

Une Grande Voix du Ciel a la France—a great voice from Heaven to France.

Lex Mercatoria—the law of commerce.

Magnalia Christi Americana—American great works of Christ.

Malachi—messenger of God.

Manuductio ad Ministerium—guidance to the ministry.

Nishmath-Chajim—the breath of life.

Parentator—one who offers a solemn sacrifice in honor of a deceased parent.

Pascentius—the herdsman, one who feeds his flock.

Pietas in Patriam—devotion to one's country; patriotism.

Psalterium Americanum—American psalter or hymn book.

Ratio Disciplinae Fratrum Nov Anglorum—system of discipline in the New England churches.

Theopolis Americana—American City of God.

SECONDARY SOURCES

1.   Biographical and Critical Studies

BERCOVITCH, SACRAN. "Cotton Mather," in Everett Emerson, ed. *Major Writers of Early American Literature*, pp. 93 - 149. Madison: University of Wisconsin Press, 1972. An extremely interesting, largely psychological approach to Cotton Mather, his beliefs, and style; special analysis and evaluation of his *Diary, Bonifacius, The Christian Philosopher*, and *Magnalia Christi Americana*.

BOAS, RALPH P. and LOUISE. *Cotton Mather, Keeper of the Puritan Conscience*. New York: Harper, 1928. An imaginative, rather than scholarly attempt to present a fair picture, with more than occasional fictionized scenes.

MARVIN, ABIJAH P. *The Life and Times of Cotton Mather*. Boston: Congregational Sunday-School & Publishing Society, 1892. A defensive account that fails to leave a clear impression; reprints valuable contemporary items.

MATHER, SAMUEL. *The Life of the Very Reverend and Learned Cotton Mather, D.D. and F.R.S.* Boston, 1729; facsimile reprint New York: Garrett Press, 1970. Biography by his son, largely based on his father's writings, especially his diaries and the Paterna, but adds a few pertinent facts; bibliographically useful for identifying (from Cotton Mather's own listing) items that had appeared anonymously.

MIDDLEKAUFF, ROBERT. *The Mathers: Three Generations of Puritan Intellectuals, 1596 - 1728*. New York: Oxford University Press, 1971. A remarkable study of the thinking of three generations of educated, religious men, based upon their writing.

MURDOCK, KENNETH B. "Cotton Mather, Parson, Scholar and Man of Affairs," in Albert Bushnell Hart, ed. *Commonwealth History of Massachusetts*, 5 vols. New York: The States History Co., 1927 - 1930. Readable, simplified, unbiased biography which attempts to see Mather in his times.

PEABODY, WILLIAM B. O. "Cotton Mather," in Jared Sparks, ed. *Library of American Biography*, Vol. VI (1836), 161 - 350; reprinted New York: Harper, 1902, Vol. XI, 3 - 190. A somewhat conventional account that shows little knowledge of Mather beyond what is to be seen in his diaries and the *Magnalia*.

QUINT, ALONZO H. "Cotton Mather," *The Congregational Quarterly*, Vol. I (1859), 233 - 64. Based on the *Diary* and on the funeral sermons delivered at Mather's death, a detailed, readable account, of especial interest as it is written from the sympathetic view of a fellow Congregational minister.

ROBBINS, CHANDLER. *A History of the Second Church, or Old North, in Boston*. Boston: John Wilson & Son, 1852. Particularly valuable for its carefully considered appraisement of the services and characters of Increase and Cotton Mather, as seen by a later occupant of their pulpit. Also has records, church documents, wills, etc.

SIBLEY, JOHN L. "Cotton Mather," *Biographical Sketches of Graduates of Harvard University*, vol. III (1885), 6 - 158. Factual, authoritative.

WENDELL, BARRETT. *Cotton Mather: The Puritan Priest*. New York: Dodd, Mead, 1891; reprinted Harcourt Brace & World, 1963. Based closely on the *Diary,* with frequent quotation, this pleasant book traditionally has been considered the best of the Mather studies, but it does little or nothing with his later work.

2. Contemporary Accounts (in addition to his son's biography)

COLMAN, BENJAMIN. *The Holy Walk and Glorious Translation of Blessed Enoch. A Sermon Preached at the Lecture in Boston, . . . after the Death of the Reverend and Learned Cotton Mather, D.D., F.R.S.* Boston, 1728. As the title indicated, Cotton Mather was one "who walked with God."

PRINCE, THOMAS. *The Departure of Elijah lamented. A Sermon Occasioned by the Great and Publick Loss In the Decease of the very Reverend & Learned Cotton Mather, D.D., F.R.S.* Boston, 1728. Cotton Mather as the "inexhaustible Source of divine Flame & Vigour."

SEWALL, SAMUEL. *Diary 1674 - 1729.* 3 vols. *Collections of Massachusetts Historical Society,* 5th ser., Vols. V - VII (1878 - 1880). Frequent comments on their shared interests (politics, antislavery propaganda, etc.), on Mather's preaching, on family affairs.

3. Essays and Articles on Individual Works or on a Phase of Cotton Mather's Work

ANDREWS, WILLIAM D. "The Printed Funeral Sermons of Cotton Mather," *Early American Literature,* Vol. V (1970), 22 - 44. Mather's fifty-five published funeral sermons, with the theme of early piety recurring frequently.

BERCOVITCH, SACRAN. "New England Epic: Cotton Mather's *Magnalia Christi Americana,*" *Journal of English Literary History,* Vol. XXXIII (1966), 337 - 50. Discusses the *Magnalia* as the "supreme achievement of American Puritan literature."

DUFFY, JOHN P. "Cotton Mather Revisited,"*Massachusetts Studies in English,* Vol. I (1967), 30 - 38. In defence of Cotton Mather, "who loved God and his neighbors, but loved God more," against his harsher critics.

GAY, PETER. *A Loss of Mastery Puritan Historians in Colonial America.* Berkeley: University of California Press, 1966. The third chapter, "Cotton Mather: A Pathetic Plutarch," is criticism of the *Magnalia* from a modern, usually unsympathetic viewpoint.

GREENE, LORENZO JOHNSTON. *The Negro in Colonial New England.* New York: Atheneum, 1969. Discusses the precedents Cotton Mather set in his efforts to Christianize the Negro.

GRISWOLD, A. WHITNEY. "Three Puritans on Prosperity," *The New England Quarterly,* Vol. VII (1934), 475 - 93. On Mather, Franklin, Dwight. Claims that Cotton Mather was laying the "true moral foundation for rugged American individualism."

HOLMES, THOMAS J. *The Mather Literature.* Cleveland, 1927. A pleasant essay on America's most prolific author, with emphasis on the inoculation controversy.

JANTZ, HAROLD S. *The First Century of New England Verse.* New York: Russell and Russell, 1962. Lists Mather's scattered poems.

LEVIN, DAVID. "The Hazing of Cotton Mather," *The New England Quarterly,* Vol. XXXVI (June 1963), 147 - 71. The very slight evidence about Cotton Mather's career as an undergraduate at Harvard.

_____. "Essays to do good for the glory of God: Cotton Mather's *Bonifacius,*" in Sacvan Bercovitch, ed. *The American Puritan Imagination. Essays in Revaluation,* pp. 139 - 55. London and New York: Cambridge University Press, 1974. (First printed as the introduction to Levin's 1966 edition of *Bonifacius.*) Especially interesting in its interpretation of Cotton Mather as a Calvinist and as a social thinker.

LOWANCE, MASON I. "Cotton Mather's *Magnalia* and the Metaphors of Biblical History," in Sacvan Bercovitch, ed. *Typology and Early American Literature,* pp. 139 - 60. Amherst: University of Massachusetts Press, 1972. Discussion of Mather's use of typology (and allegory and metaphor), sources and purpose.

MACLEAR, J. F. "New England and the Fifth Monarchy: The Quest for the Millennium in Early American Puritanism," *William and Mary Quarterly,* 3rd series, Vol. XXXII (April 1975), pp. 223 - 60. A brief history of the millennium tradition, so dominant in the thinking of the Cottons and the Mathers.

MANIERRE, WILLIAM R. II. "Cotton Mather and the Biographical Parallel," *American Quarterly,* Vol. XII (1961), 153 - 60.

_____. "Some Characteristic Mather Redactions," *The New England Quarterly,* Vol. XXXI (1958), 496 - 505.

_____. "Verbal Patterns in Cotton Mather's *Magnalia,*" *Quarterly Journal of Speech,* Vol. XLVII (1961), 403 - 13. Three analyses of Cotton Mather's style.

_____. "A Description of 'Paterna': The Unpublished Autobiography of Cotton Mather," *Studies in Bibliography,* Vol. XVIII (1965), 183 - 205. Mather's almost complete dependence on his diaries for the autobiography.

MURDOCK, KENNETH B. "Cotton Mather and the Rectorship of Yale College," *Publications Colonial Society of Massachusetts,* Vol. XXVI (1927), 388 - 401. The evidence that Cotton Mather was offered the rectorship (presidency) of Yale.

_____. *Increase Mather the Foremost American Puritan.* Cambridge: Harvard University Press, 1925. This life of Cotton Mather's father is extremely useful for its information about Cotton Mather, its interpretation of the Mather tradition of piety and service, and its discussion of the relation of the Mathers to the politics of their time (Chapters XIII - XV)

_____. Introduction, *Selections from Cotton Mather,* pp. ix - lxiii. New

York: Hafner, 1926. An extremely valuable consideration of Cotton Mather as a scholar and man of letters, followed by significant introductory information about the *Magnalia Christi Americana*, *The Christian Philosopher*, and the *Political Fables*.

NEWLIN, CLAUDE M. *Philosophy and Religion in Colonial America*. New York: Philosophical Library, 1962. Begins with Mather's *The Christian Philosopher* and *Manuductio ad Ministerium* as the first American books to try to reconcile the new science and religion.

QUINCY, JOSIAH P. "Cotton Mather and the Supernormal in New England History," *Massachusetts Historical Society Proceedings*, ser. 2, Vol. XX (1906), 439 - 53. A defense of Cotton Mather, as in some eras there is far more recognition of the supernatural than in other periods.

RICE, HOWARD C. "Cotton Mather Speaks to France. American Propaganda in the Age of Louis XIV," *The New England Quarterly*, Vol. XVI (1943), 198 - 233. Interesting article as it places Mather's efforts to convert Roman Catholics in France (and Spain) and to save the French Protestant churches in the international events of the period.

SENSABAUCH, GEORGE. *Milton in Early America*. Princeton: Princeton University Press, 1964. The second chapter discusses the influence of Milton on Mather.

SHEA, DANIEL B. *Spiritual Autobiography in Early America*. Princeton: Princeton University Press, 1968. Includes a sensitive consideration of Mather's Paterna, and the relationship of the Paterna, the *Diary*, and *Bonifacius*.

SMITH, PETER H. "Politics and Sainthood: Biography by Cotton Mather," *William and Mary Quarterly*, 3rd series, Vol. XX (1963), 186 - 206. Argues that the biographies in the *Magnalia* were much influenced by political considerations.

TUTTLE, JULIUS. H. "The Libraries of the Mathers," *Proceedings American Antiquarian Society*, n.s. Vol. XX (1910), 269 - 356.

TYLER, MOSES COIT. *A History of American Literature, 1607 - 1765*. 2 vols. New York: Putnam, 1878; rev. ed. 1897. Still standard and of interest, especially for its evaluation of style.

VARTANIAN, PERSHING. "Cotton Mather and the Puritan Transition into the Enlightenment," *Early American Literature*, Vol. VII (1972), 213 - 24. The shifting from Puritanism to Rationalism not a matter of contrasts but of emphasis.

WARREN, AUSTIN. "Grandfather Mather and his Wonder Book," *Sewanee Review*, Vol. LXXII (1964), 96 - 116. The *Magnalia* as history and as baroque prose.

————. *The New England Conscience*. Ann Arbor: University of Michigan Press, 1966. Has chapter on Cotton Mather's conscience as revealed in the *Diary*, pp. 76 - 87.

WEEKS, LOUIS III. "Cotton Mather and the Quakers," *Quaker History*, Vol. LIX (1970), pp. 24 - 33. Early vituperative harshness gave way to a search for axioms of common doctrine.

WHITE, EUGENE E. "Cotton Mather's *Manuductio ad Ministerium,"* *Quarterly Journal of Speech,* Vol. XLIX (1963), 308 - 19. On Mather's stylistic habits in the *Manuductio.*

WOODY, KENNERLY M. "Cotton Mather's *Manuductio ad Theologium*: The "More Quiet and Hopeful Way," *Early American Literature,* Vol. IV, No. 2, pp. 3 - 48. On the influence of German pietism and the practices of the University of Halle on Mather's suggested curriculum.

―――――. "Bibliographical Notes on Cotton Mather's *Manuductio ad Ministerium,"* *Early American Literature,* Vol. VI supplement, 1 - 98. Identifies Mather's suggested readings for young ministers-to-be.

4. Cotton Mather and Pietism

BENZ, ERNST. "Ecumenical Relations between Boston Puritanism and German Pietism: Cotton Mather and August Hermann Francke," *Harvard Theological Review,* Vol. LIV (1961), 159 - 93.

―――――. "Pietist and Puritan Sources of Early Protestant Missions (Cotton Mather and August Hermann Francke)," *Church History,* Vol. XXI (1951), 28 - 55.

FRANCKE, KUNO. "The Beginnings of Cotton Mather's Correspondence with August Hermann Francke," *Philosophical Quarterly,* Vol. V (1929), 193 - 95.

―――――. "Cotton Mather and August Hermann Francke," *Harvard Studies in Philosophy and Literature,* Vol. V (1896), 57 - 67.

―――――. "Further Documents concerning Cotton Mather and August Hermann Francke," *Americana Germanica,* Vol. I (1897), No. 4, pp. 31 - 66.

SHIPTON, CLIFFORD. "Literary Leaven in Provincial New England," *The New England Quarterly,* Vol. IX (1936), 203 - 17. The influence of contemporary German religious thought on Cotton Mather.

5. Cotton Mather and the New Science

BEALL, OTHO T. JR., and RICHARD H. SHRYOCK. *Cotton Mather, First Significant Figure in American Medicine.* Baltimore: Johns Hopkins Press, 1954. Mather's contribution to American medicine is discussed clearly and in detail; also valuable for its consideration of Mather as a source of information about the medical thought of his day.

BLAKE, JOHN. "The Inoculation Controversy in Boston, 1721 - 1722," *New England Quarterly,* XXV (1952), 489 - 506. Often cited as the most objective account of the smallpox controversy.

HORNBERGER, THEODORE. "The Date, the Source, and the Significance of Cotton Mather's Interest in Science," *American Literature,* VI (1935), 413 - 20.

―――――. "Science and the New World," *Catalogue of the Huntington Library* (1937), pp. 318. Stresses the Mathers (and Winthrops).

KING, LESTER S. *The Road to Medical Enlightenment 1650 - 1695.* London:

MacDonald, 1970. Excellent study of the conflicting philosophical and biological theories of the period.

KITTREDGE, GEORGE LYMAN. "Cotton Mather's Election into the Royal Society," *Publications of the Colonial Society of Massachusetts*, XIV (1913), 81 - 114.

————. "Cotton Mather's Scientific Communications to the Royal Society," *Proceedings* of the American Antiquarian Society, n.s., XXVI (1916), 18 - 57. Identifies and annotates each communication.

————. "Further Notes on Cotton Mather and the Royal Society, *Pub. Col. Soc. Mass.*, XIV (1913), 281 - 92.

————. "Some Lost Works of Cotton Mather," *Proceedings*, Massachusetts Historical Society, XLV (1922), 418 - 79. The inoculation controversy.

STEARNS, RAYMOND PHINEAS. *Science in the British Colonies of America.* Urbana: University of Illinois, 1970. Devotes some chapters to Cotton Mather and his contemporaries, and so considers Mather in the perspective of his times.

WINSLOW, OLA ELIZABETH. *A Destroying Angel: The Conquest of Smallpox in Colonial Boston.* Boston: Houghton Mifflin, 1974. A very readable book that tells much about medical practice in the eighteenth century both before and after Cotton Mather and Dr. Zabdiel Boylston succeeded in starting the use of inoculation.

ZIRKLE, CONWAY. *The Beginning of Plant Hybridization.* Philadelphia: University of Pennsylvania Press, 1935. Includes Cotton Mather's report to the Royal Society, the initial observation of this process.

6. Cotton Mather and Witchcraft

CALEF, ROBERT. *More Wonders of the Invisible World, or The Wonders of the Invisible World Displayed in Five Parts.* London, 1700; reprinted Salem, 1823. A confused attack on the Mathers, especially Cotton. Includes the surreptitious printing of Cotton Mather's.

HOLMES, THOMAS J. "Cotton Mather and His Writings on Witchcraft," *Papers of the Bibliographical Society of America*, Vol. XVIII (1925), 30 - 59.

————. "The Surreptitious Printing of one of Cotton Mather's Manuscripts," in *Bibliographical Essays: A Tribute to Wilberforce Eames*, 1925, pp. 149 - 60.

HANSEN, CHADWICK. *Witchcraft at Salem.* New York: New American Library, 1970. Disproves many of the nineteenth-century fallacies about what had actually taken place in Massachusetts.

KITTREDGE, GEORGE LYMAN. *Witchcraft in Old and New England.* New York: Russell & Russell, 1956. The standard work on the history of witchcraft, with a one-chapter analysis of the outbreak in New England.

LEVIN, DAVID. *What Happened in Salem? Documents Pertaining to the*

Seventeenth Century Witchcraft Trials. New York: Harcourt, Brace & World, 1960. Valuable for its reprinting (for five cases) the actual trial testimonies, documents, and other contemporary narratives.

WERKING, RICHARD H. " 'Reformation is our Only Preservation': Cotton Mather and Salem Witchcraft," *William and Mary Quarterly*, 3rd series, Vol. XXIX (April 1972), 281 - 90. An interesting consideration of Mather's difficult position in 1692: his duty to protect the judges' reputations, his desire to have the reality of witchcraft recognized (as part of the spiritual world), and his conscientious wish to protect the possibly innocent.

7. Background Studies
   (Selected as important for understanding Cotton Mather)

BAILYN, BERNARD. *The New England Merchants in the Seventeenth Century.* New York: Harper Torchbook, 1964. A carefully documented and organized study of economic and political changes in New England.

BERNSTEIN, HENRY. *Origins of Inter-American Interest 1700 - 1812.* Philadelphia: University of Pennsylvania Press, 1945. Discusses at some length the influence of Cotton Mather and Samuel Sewall in developing interest in Spanish-American affairs.

BERCOVITCH, SACVAN. *Horologicals to Chronometricals. The Rhetoric of the Jeremiad.* Madison: University of Wisconsin Press, 1970. *Literary Monographs*, Vol. 3, pp. 1 - 124. Of particular value for an understanding of millennarian beliefs, so fervid in the seventeenth century.

BRIDENBAUGH, CARL. *Cities in the Wilderness. The First Century of Urban Life in America, 1625 - 1742.* London and New York: Oxford University Press, 1971 (copr. 1938). A scholarly and disinterested survey of changing social, economic, and political conditions in Boston (and other seaboard cities).

CRAGG, C.R. *From Puritanism to the Age of Reason.* Cambridge: Cambridge University Press, 1966. While the author's main interest is Puritanism within the Church of England, this study has pertinent chapters discussing the effect on religious thinking of the new interest in science.

CREMIN, LAWRENCE A. *American Education: The Colonial Experience, 1607 - 1783.* New York: Harper & Row, 1970. Discusses Mather's erudition, his belief that piety is the chief end of education, his establishing the communal character of good works.

ELLIOTT, EMORY. *Power and the Pulpit in Puritan New England.* Princeton, N.J.: Princeton University Press, 1975.

LOVE, WILLIAM DE L. *The Fast and Thanksgiving Days of New England.* Boston: Houghton, Mifflin, 1895. A standard introduction to Puritan practices.

MERIWETHER, COLYER. *Our Colonial Curriculum 1607 - 1776.* Washington,

D.C.: Capital Publishing Co., 1907. Still very informative, covering various phases of the Harvard curriculum (languages, mathematics, religion, science).

MILLER, PERRY. *The New England Mind: From Colony to Province*. Cambridge, Mass.: Harvard University Press, 1953. Quietly and perniciously anti-Mather, although Mather's accomplishments are acknowledged. (For many years the late Perry Miller's books have been regarded as authoritative and learned treatises on Puritan thinking and literature, for which all students should be grateful; of late years there have been timid suggestions that some of his views could be reconsidered.)

MORAIS, HERBERT M. *Deism in Eighteenth Century America*. New York: Columbia University Press, 1934. Considers Cotton Mather to be the first American deist.

MORGAN, EDMUND S. *The Puritan Family. Religion and Domestic Relations in Seventeenth-Century New England*. New York: Harper, 1944; Harper Torchbook, 1966. The effect of Puritan beliefs on daily life, family relationships, theories of education; based on contemporary journals and sermons, with Cotton Mather a frequent source.
Visible Saints. The History of a Puritan Idea. New York: New York University Press, 1963. The early Puritan theory of the church of the Elect and later developments, including the Half-Way Covenant.

MORISON, SAMUEL ELIOT. *Harvard College in the Seventeenth Century*. 2 vols. Cambridge, Mass.: Harvard University Press, 1936. The Harvard of 1650 - 1708, including chapters on the curriculum, students, finances, presidents; a comprehensive study, filled with valuable information, by one of Harvard's most distinguished scholars, but some questions have been raised about the author's objectivity.
————. *The Intellectual Life of Colonial New England*. New York: New York University Press, 1956 (2nd ed.). Very readable and informative lectures on different phases of New England culture: education, printing, libraries, literature, et al.

MURDOCK, KENNETH. *Literature and Theology in Colonial New England*. New York: Harper & Row, 1963. An essay, written with the usual Murdock charm, on "the relation between the New England Puritans' fundamental theological ideas and their literary theory and practice."

POPE, ROBERT G. *The Half-Way Covenant. Church Membership in Puritan New England*. Princeton: Princeton University Press, 1969. A remarkably clear analysis of Puritan theories on church membership; based on primary material: church records, diaries, sermons, etc.

RILEY, I. WOODBRIDGE. *American Philosophy: The Early Schools*. New York: Dodd, Mead, 1907.
American Thought from Puritanism to Pragmatism and Beyond. New York: Dodd, Mead, 1915; Gloucester, Mass., Peter Smith, 1941. Still standard and useful.

SEYBOLT, ROBERT FRANCIS. *The Public Schools of Boston 1635 - 1775*. Cambridge, Mass.: Harvard University Press, 1935. Discusses the practical side of the establishment of the schools, their support, their masters as well as the curriculum. Includes Cotton Mather's concern for the establishment and improvement of public schools.

SHIPTON, CLIFFORD K. "The New England Clergy of the 'Glacial Age,'" *Publications of the Colonial Society of Massachusetts*, XXXII (1937), 24 - 54. A plea against accepting stereotypes.

SWEET, WILLIAM WARREN. *Religion in Colonial America*. New York: Scribner's, 1942. A standard one-volume history, very clear and unbiased.

SWIFT, LINDSAY. "The Massachusetts Election Sermons," *Publications of the Colonial Society of Massachusetts*, Vol. I (1895), 388 - 451. Stresses Cotton Mather's early voice (in his four Election Day sermons) against the slave trade and for temperance.

WALKER, WILLISTON. *A History of the Congregational Churches in the United States*. (American Church History Series). New York: Christian Literature Co., 1894. The influence of the Second Church and Cotton Mather on church polity.

WILLIAMS, STANLEY T. *The Spanish Background of American Literature*. 2 vols. New Haven: Yale University Press, 1955. Cotton Mather's learning Spanish the beginning of the study of Spanish by scholars.

WRIGHT, THOMAS G. *Literary Culture in Early New England, 1620 - 1730*. New Haven: Yale University Press, 1920. A survey of Puritan reading.

ZIFF, LARZER. *Puritanism in America New Culture in a New World*. New York: Viking, 1973. The interrelationship of changes in politics, economics, society, religion, literature.

Index

186